CP 10^u

kenzo tange

kenzo tange

Paolo Riani

Hamlyn
London   New York   Sydney   Toronto

twentieth-century masters
General editors: H. L. Jaffé and A. Busignani

© Copyright in the text Sadea/Sansoni, Florence, 1969
© Copyright in the illustrations Paolo Riani
Drawings and photographs of models supplied by Kenzo Tange's studio
© Copyright this edition The Hamlyn Publishing Group Limited 1970
London · New York · Sydney · Toronto
Hamlyn House, Feltham, Middlesex, England
ISBN 0 600 35302 8

Colour lithography Zincotipia Moderna, Florence
Printing and binding: Cox and Wyman Limited
London, Fakenham and Reading

Distributed in the United States of America by Crown Publishers Inc.

contents

List of colour illustrations

List of black-and-white illustrations

Hiroshima: heroic testimony

The end of the Second World War left Japan in the worst state it had been in during the whole of its history. Destruction was everywhere, the larger towns—Tokyo, Nagoya, Kyoto, Hiroshima—transformed by conflagration into lunar landscapes, endless panoramas of ashen waste.

'I cannot dispel from my memory the image of the city (Tokyo) as I saw it immediately after the war, at the end of 1945 . . . The spectacle that met my eyes was desolate . . . Around Marunouchi, the financial centre of the metropolis, a few of the larger reinforced concrete structures still stood upright . . . but vast areas of homes, small shops and stores in lower Tokyo had been completely razed to the ground.

'Here there were not even the mountains of rubble of German towns; the wooden structures had gone up in flames and smoke, leaving the ground covered with black dust and spent embers.

'For acres and acres the prospect was one of a grey desert, where every now and then one came across broken crockery, strange green stones (the remains of bottles that had molten because of the heat), misshapen sheets of corrugated iron which had barely been covered by some flowering climber that had managed to germinate between one bombing and the next . . .

'Few know that the terrible saturation bombing, from March to May of that year, did more damage and produced more casualties than the atom bomb at Hiroshima. For instance the bombing of 9th–10th March began in the evening around 10.30 and lasted all night, several hundred B–29 bombers dropped thousands of tons of explosive and incendiary bombs on the lower areas of the city. The conflagration, fanned by a strong wind, spread furiously: the day after, all that remained of the most crowded quarter of Tokyo, a honeycomb of houses, shops, stores, public buildings and small factories, was a flattened smoking zone where everything had been incinerated.

'Counting the dead was always difficult in situations such as this: how many bodies had been burnt to a cinder by that intense heat?

'The official documents number the dead and missing as 124,711—a figure much larger than that of the massacre of Hiroshima.'

But much more serious is the moral discomfiture that follows such a defeat, like the sense of shock which follows a frightening experience or great labour whose consequences are only realised after the danger has passed or the work completed.

'. . . Why was the losing of the war such a catastrophe for the Japanese? The explanation is not hard to find—for two thousand years the archipelago had never been invaded and occupied by any enemy, nor had Japanese troops ever been defeated by a foreign power. So losing the war meant a re-thinking of fundamental attitudes towards existence and the world as a whole: it was almost as though one of nature's basic laws had been shown to be false . . .

'The day on which the Emperor announced the decision to surrender seemed if not the end of the world, at least the end of a world. There were many suicides, some fifty before the Imperial palace itself, but the vast majority of the Japanese people who had survived faced the changed situation with an attitude of stunned passivity and spiritual surrender.'

It was at this time that the concept of democracy, which had no precedent in Japan, was introduced there.

Hiroshima became a symbol in the drive for reconstruction. The will for a new start was combined with the desire to wipe out the memory of mankind's darkest hour.[1] A competition for a Peace Park[2] was instituted and was won by a design that was simple, forthright and without rhetoric.

Its architect was Kenzo Tange, a young man whose work had matured through various styles between the Wars. His graduating thesis, a design for a Palace of the Arts, was strictly rationalist and gained him the Tatsuno prize given yearly for graduates of Tokyo University. In contrast, four years later in 1942 he won the competition for the Daitoa Kensetsu Memorial with a design that owed much to the revivalism that was then in fashion.

Tange then studied with Kunio Mayekawa and his experience in his studio conditioned many of his attitudes.[3] Kunio Mayekawa, together with Junzo Sakakura, had effectively brought the modern movement to Japan through the teachings of Le Corbusier, with whom he had worked for a long time in the Rue de Sèvres studio in Paris.

When Tange entered for the Hiroshima competition, he was already well-known for a controversial design for a dwelling-house in Tokyo,[4] in which he had blended rationalist methodology with Japanese forms.

The nature of the Hiroshima project placed it above controversy. 'This Peace Park,' Tange said, 'is not that heart of an ideal city to which we have been mentally so attached. It represents an unusual and fortunate oppor-

---

1 'On the 6th August, 1945, the town of Hiroshima experienced the most fearful destruction man has ever known. Slowly and gradually the idea has been erased from the minds of those who survived that terrible judgement of the Lord that the world faces a problem that surpasses all others. The unleashing of atomic energy can either advance the well-being of the human race at an unprecedented pace or else totally destroy all that there is on earth. A single factor will determine which alternative will prevail: whether we have peace or war. The people of Hiroshima have decided in unison to put themselves on the side of peace and to show that to the world. The physical appearance of the town where the people of Hiroshima will live shall be a monument to perpetual peace. The sincere and resolute purpose of this community has been noted by the National Diet which passed the "Law for the Construction of the City of Hiroshima for the Commemoration of Peace" on the 6th August, 1949, on the fourth anniversary of that fatal day.' (From an address by the Mayor of Hiroshima.)

2 The programme for the reconstruction of the City of Peace was spread over fifteen years and comprised: (1) the project for the Hall of Peace, consisting of the construction of a hall to seat 2,500 people, the Peace Square, which could hold 20,000, an Arch of Peace with bells, and a commemorative chapel housed in the ruins of a domed building destroyed by the atomic explosion. (2) The project for the Peace Park comprising a Children's Centre (a hall for 1,500 children, a library, a museum, a club-house, a swimming-pool etc.). (3) The Peace Avenue and a number of bridges: this avenue, a hundred metres wide will be the most grandiose in Japan, with gardens surrounding it. Also the bridges at Hiroshima, which is crossed in several different directions by seven waterways, represent much more than links between the various parts of the town. (4) International hotels and dormitories located in the most beautiful parts of the city.

3 'The generation of Tange and Oe is the generation which studied modern architecture of the West on paper while their surrounding world was resounding with war-time propaganda for nationalism.

When Japan lost the war and towns and cities had been totally destroyed, Tange and Oe appeared with their theories. It was through their efforts that the modern architecture of the West was translated into Japanese form. But gradually, with the experience acquired by building temporary shacks in burnt-down areas or drawing detailed designs of minimum-cost buildings, a new generation of architects emerged. The time had come for that generation, which had directly absorbed democratic education amidst the post-war labour movement and the student movement (and not the generation which had argued for the democratisation of Japan), to speak up on a social basis. Masako Otaka, Azusa Kito and other architects belonging to the Mido group of Kunio Mayekawa, who advocated the adoption of the technical approach, are representative members of this generation . . . The above-mentioned discovery of a new method of introducing the concept of labour and material was carried out by these architects. And Kenzo Tange is at present of the same opinion.' (Noboru Kawazoe, 'Modern Japanese Architecture Confronts Functionalism. New Buildings in Japan', in Zodiac, No. 3, pp. 116–148.)

2. Peace Park, Hiroshima, 1947:
Detail of the overall plan

3. Katsura Imperial Palace,
Kyoto (17th century)

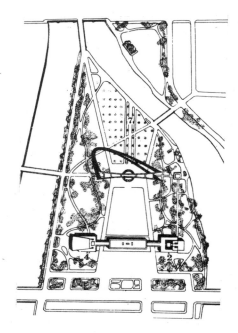

tunity in Japan. For it has been possible to gain the co-operation of various administrative and governing interests and get them to agree to act together as a single body so that the realisation of this project may be possible. There are still two schools of thought at Hiroshima: some believe that this project should not be undertaken so long as there are still homeless: others hold that the two forms of reconstruction should proceed side by side. We think that the special situation in which Hiroshima is now in the eyes of the world justifies the construction of this Project for Peace, along with the reconstruction of housing.'

Here, too, the architectural forms were still those of Le Corbusier– raised on columns *(pilotis)*, like the Swiss Pavilion in Paris in 1937, openplan, glass walls (the *plan de verrure*), sun-breakers (the *brise-soleil*) and reinforced concrete *(béton brut)* . . . but these are relived and translated– with a surprising confidence–into an expressive language that managed to reflect the stupefied grief and awed shock of the eye-witness.[5] The project was widely known and assumed the importance of a sign-post at a moment when a modern style was being sought in the architecture of Japan.

The name of Kenzo Tange became linked with those of better-known architects, like Kunio Mayekawa and Junzo Sakakura, who after twenty years of vainly promoting the cause of rationalist architecture, found themselves in the cultural leadership of the new generations who set about the task of reconstruction.

During the following years Tange built several buildings which, although they were architecturally extremely competent, did not reach the level of the Hiroshima Centre and remained well below the better works of the great Japanese architects at that time, like Gakshuin's University or Mayekawa's Tokyo Festival Hall.

For Tange the Children's Library in Hiroshima (1951), the Ehime Conference Centre at Matsuyama (1952), the City Hall of Shimizu (1953), the College Library at Tsuda (1953), the Printing Press at Nomazu (1954–5), the City Hall at Kurayoshi (1955), the Conference Building at Shizuoka (1955) and the Sumi Memorial (1955) are so many stages in his rapid progression to architectural maturity.[6]

4 'Nevertheless in this almost artless, primitive-looking house, it may be that Tange was more reluctant to express the complex realities of modern Japan than he was later in some of his more recent monumental works. In spite of this, he seems to have attained a dynamic balance in this work between the various contradictions which he involves himself with, in particular that between creativity and tradition. The fact that this small building is one of his most successful gives it unusual prominence. Besides, this is his own house, and the house of an architect (whether he had designed it all himself, or only lived in it) is surely most indicative of his thinking and his personality.' (Robin Boyd: *Kenzo Tange,* New York, Braziller, 1962.)

5 'One of Tange's most important works is the Peace Park at Hiroshima. The town itself is today a sorry conglomeration of bombed areas and new commercial and residential quarters, built in a hurry, which excel even our commercial buildings in ugliness, for the finance available is extremely limited and there is relatively little experience in the use of modern constructional techniques. The situation of the town is uniquely beautiful. It stands in the middle of a wide delta formed by the eight channels of a river as it empties into the sea and is surrounded by high mountains. The Peace Park, which covers a vast area, is so far composed of a civic centre, an exhibition pavilion and a museum. A short distance away from these buildings is the monument to the victims of the A bomb. This is an expressive sculpture in reinforced concrete that recalls the form of the simple prehistoric Japanese house, whose form is recorded in some clay models that were discovered in tombs. Its curved shape forms an elegant contrast with the straight, horizontal lines of the other buildings. The details are worked with a refinement that is difficult to achieve in Western countries.

These are the real and relevant values I hold dear and want to share with others. I am convinced that the lover of art and architecture has a great deal to gain from a visit to Japan. Here he will find complete and sublime solutions to the complicated problems of space and human scale–the real means for the expression of architectural creativity.' (Walter Gropius, from the preface to the book by Kenzo Tange, with photography by Yasuhiro Ishimoto, *Katsura: Tradition and Creation in Japanese Architecture,* New Haven, Yale University Press, 1960.)

6 An analysis of these early works by Tange is not made in this study, for it was felt that the points that they made appear again in more mature form in the later works. For a detailed description and sensitive analysis of these designs, the reader is referred to Robin Boyd's *Kenzo Tange,* while their place in a broader perspective is well described in Noboru Kawazoe's *Contemporary Japanese Architecture,* 1965, which is basic to the understanding of the development of modern architecture in a background such as that of Japan. 'On the other hand the works of this transitional period emanate the professionalism that came to be part of his work, detracting perhaps from his methodological pursuits. They are competent and precise, clear and efficient, and to a certain extent diagrammatic. They have the merit of being neither humble nor ostentatious in their scale and in the relationship of their structural parts. These are, then, works which are certainly not pretentious;

4. Ici Riki, Kyoto.
Geisha house in the
Ghion quarter (Edo period)

In his search for new expressive forms, Tange reviews all the stages in the development of the modern movement. His conscious rejection of tradition means that he sometimes adopts elements of expression that are foreign to his own nature. Sometimes these appear as echoes of his experience of other architecture from abroad. His town halls at Shimizu and Tokyo show the influence of Mies van der Rohe and the buildings at Nomazu and Shizuoka that of Le Corbusier.[7] Such influences—apart from their justification on technological grounds—stem from the ever more rapid spread of stylistic elements that is part of the continual renewal of modern architecture. Tange is above duplicity. His deliberate choice of stylistic elements is not irresponsible but rather a means of association that can facilitate real methodological progress.

His architecture was certainly of high quality and on the level of imagery the influence was not all one way, for it soon became a close exchange between two cultures.[8]

Tange's great community buildings

Pls. 12–15
Figs. 11–15
Pls. 23–8
Figs. 16–19

The various elements which make up what Tange is seeking to achieve may be understood through the analysis of two extremely interesting buildings that were designed and erected in the second half of the 1950s. These are the Kagawa Prefectural Office (1959) and the Kurashiki City Hall (1960). These are great community buildings, which owe their conception to the need to identify the new forms of community life, and their creation is based on an act of faith, a form of invention entirely disassociated from any cultural precedent. They emanate the resolve behind the new force of democracy, in contrast to more traditional forms, and among the extraordinary number of public buildings constructed in Japan through a well-defined government programme they come to symbolise the new spirit of partnership. The spatial distribution is still the same as the 1952 City Hall in Tokyo,[9] but it is more clearly and fully worked out, exemplifying the efforts of the whole nation towards a reconstruction on new, democratic lines. This is in itself a lesson for the West, the fatherland of democracy, which since the era of the communes has been unable to create space of this nature.

Pls. 8, 9
Fig. 20

Pls. 8, 13, 14, 23, 24

The organisation of the space is in three parts. On the ground level the building is raised off the ground on *pilotis,* so the space is interpreted as an extension of the open air, through which one may circulate freely.

they are modest and full of caution—but convincingly right when they are considered against the formal background they belong to.' (Robin Boyd, *op. cit.*)

7 'Rationalism presented considerable advantages—particularly that of creating a common platform that allowed for the effective exchange of experience within a movement that was collective in more senses than one. To progress with experiments that had been started involved above all else continuity with the common platform, which for the Japanese already possessed a distinctive character and represented something to preserve. Kenzo Tange had already moved in this direction with his Tokyo City Hall, although the building was completed late so far as the internal cultural situation was concerned—in the meantime other initiatives for architectural expression had been tried out along lines that differed substantially from those that Tange and Mayekawa had already clearly defined.' (Manfredo Tafuri, *L'Architettura moderna in Giappone,* Bologna, 1964.) Study of Tafuri is still basic to the understanding of the complex situation in which Japanese architects came to be working and of the place that Tange's work has in a wider context.

8 'Between 1920 and 1930 the avant-garde architecture was German; in the period immediately after the War the sirens of fashion dusted their *art nouveau* forms; towards 1950 we witnessed the fleeting impact of the Brasilian explosion; today we can see, just as then in the work of German architects, that it is the Japanese who have the most relevant architectural message, even though it may not be as revolutionary as that of the former . . .

That Japanese architecture was by nature more suited to the acceptance of modernism which might be to a certain extent prefigured in the refined and precise rationality of the arrangement of the Japanese house is an old idea which cannot be ignored . . . but which we find a hasty and insufficient explanation.

For Ragghianti, Japanese architecture is intensely involved in what we have already had the opportunity of calling "nostalgia for the future"—preoccupied in the pursuit of universal language.

This is perhaps even too obvious in some examples, which are more or less utopian . . . like Arata Isozaki's Air City, Kiyonori Kikutake's Marina City, the fair-like Miyakojo Communal Building by the same architect, or some of the pavilions planned for the 1970 Osaka World Fair.

But it is also equally obvious that some of the more technically and formally complete and mature expressions—from Tange to Sakakura and Mayekawa—must be seen as a sort of extraordinary, even futuristic and sometimes overwhelming extrapolation of the very innermost Japanese spirit.' (Agnoldomenico Pica, 'Una Mostra e un congresso a Firenze. Architettura giapponese contemporanea', in *Domas,* 474, May, 1969.)

The purpose of this space is made evident through a series of elements that have a collective function and it is directly linked, by means of a group of elevators, to the upper part of the building and the roof garden *(le toit jardin)* whose function is also community-orientated. The offices are arranged according to strictly functional criteria on the floors in between.

This structure was warmly appreciated by the public. A year and a half after the inauguration, as much as a sixth of the population of the prefectural district had visited the roof garden and made use of the facilities at Takamatsu, the Prefectural headquarters at Kagawa. 'The understanding of reality is reflected in us in our thinking and in our way of life,' Tange was later to say. 'This naturally involves a political choice, as soon as one realises that architecture inevitably reflects the political achievements of a society and in turn engenders others. No one would deny that housing and town-planning are topics that have political implications. In spite of this, it is no solution for the architect simply to become politically involved. The most appropriate attitude for him to adopt is to be architecturally alive, to try to grasp and give form to the reality of society in his architectural creation, to approach reality from the point of view of architecture.

'However much reality is outside us, it is reflected within us. It is this inner reality that is given form through the process of architectural creation.'

These works, symbolic of the new partnership in Japanese life,[10] soon became a point of reference for other buildings of a similar kind, for other communities in other cities.[11] But in these buildings the architectural

---

9 It was thought appropriate wherever possible to examine the ideas behind Tange's work through his own writings, which themselves present the clearest explanations of his processes of architectural creation. We are of the opinion that the outlining of the direction and method, study and progress is more important than the evaluation of the finished product, especially as some of Tange's works are extremely inviting and features in them may have an artificial and transient circulation without contributing to any methodological progress: 'It seems to us that the City Hall should once again return to its original function, that is to summon the people to common effort. Now this tradition has never existed in Japan, where buildings such as these represented above all power. We have wanted as architects to assist the people to this new consciousness by making of this group of buildings around the Tokyo City Hall the veritable "spiritual centre" of our capital. So the entrance hall, which is not monumental even though its dimensions may be large, serves the function of welcoming the public, and the gallery on the mezzanine floor, which is reserved for pedestrians, forming a link between the building and the city, fulfills the same psychological function–to invite the public to group themselves around the symbol of the city itself.' (Kenzo Tange, The Tokyo City Hall, in *L'Architecture d'Aujourd'hui*, No. 82, 1959, p. 89.)

10 'While Japan had accustomed us to refined combinations between ancient and modern, these bold and simple designs, that are nevertheless full of energy and meaning, point the way to a promising cultural revival. The rigorous tradition of Japanese architecture, seen in the domination of the notions of *Zoka* and *Kenchiku*, is broken.

The current movement is only one facet of the great effort that is under way to develop Japanese society in a democratic fashion and its fate depends on the global success of that effort. It is nonetheless true that Tange and the others have a very powerful impulse behind them, and one which seems capable of surmounting a great number of obstacles.

Their experience has a lesson in methodology for us all. It places us on our guard against those facile and idealistic theories for the reconciliation of ancient and modern, in the presence of an illustrious tradition that is still rooted in the minds of the majority. While modern architectural thinking is able to recognise the external and picturesque values from those that have real substance, recognising the modernity of the traditional Japanese house with its unified decoration, its established links between the interior and the exterior, its inherent capacity for expansion on organic lines, the young Japanese architects have realised that it is impossible to insist on the preservation of that harmony that is inseparably linked to a series of social conditions and limitations that are unacceptable today.' (Leonardo Benevolo, 'Il Giappone', in *Storia dell'Architettura Moderna*, Cap. XIX, 'Il nuovo ambiente internazionale', p. 1019, Vol. II, ed. Laterza, Bari, 1960.)

11 We were struck by the extraordinary proportion of 'types' in contemporary Japanese architecture–which we may roughly divide into those that are private and those that have public interest.

The Japanese architect, far more than his Western counterpart, seems to be wholly absorbed in fulfilling the needs of three categories of clients (1) the rich class (for whom he designs houses and recreational facilities such as luxury hotels, bathing establishments, clubs, golf courses, swimming pools, etc.) (2) the big industrial and business firms (production facilities, scientific research establishments, large offices, big stores, stations, theatres, sports arenas, etc.) (3) Government and administrative authorities (town halls, administrative offices, police buildings, ministries, the state universities, hospitals, etc.).

The public emerges as the beneficiary in many of the instances in the summary list above, but in the role of a passive consumer, an indispensable element in the production machine which does not contribute, except minimally, to increased welfare.

We should also note that the architectural themes that have become so prominent in recent years in the so-called 'welfare states' (housing, neighbourhood facilities, homes for the invalid and the old, schools at all levels) are much rarer; taking into account the size of the country and the population (almost a hundred millions) it can be said that such facilities are almost non-existent. (*Casabella-Continuità*, No. 273, March, 1963.)

6. Riohanji garden, Kyoto
(16th century)

**Continuity and meaning
of tradition**

process of creation is directed towards the refinement rather than the development of the theme, and the force and authenticity of the form is diminished proportionately to the amount salvaged from the immense Japanese cultural inheritance.

Close attention should be given to the different architectural forms that form the background, at Kagawa and Kurashiki, to the same spatial organisation. Apart from being fundamental to Tange's work as a whole, they also clarify his position with regard to tradition and mark his place in a continuing cultural development.

'I became interested in Japanese tradition a good many years ago, and since that time have read a number of history books and seen as many architectural relics as possible', Tange wrote in an explanatory presentation of the Kagawa Prefectural Office.[12] 'My study has led me to the conclusion that tradition can no longer continue under its own impetus and that it cannot be considered to generate creative energy. To be transformed into something creative, tradition must be denied and, in a sense, destroyed. Instead of being apotheosised, it must be desecrated.

'The question that has interested me particularly is whether in Japanese history one can actually find traces of the iconoclastic energy necessary to transform tradition into something new. The history of Japan, compared to that of other nations, is rather uneventful. There have been no sweeping revolutions, even in the cultural sphere, and on the face of it the energy in question seems relatively weak.

Fig. 3

'The period from the fifteenth to the seventeenth century is exceptionally interesting in this connection, for this was an age when new social patterns developed, and when new aspirations were expressed in Japanese art and architecture. The Katsura Palace will serve as an excellent example of the esthetic ideals which prevailed in the latter part of this period. The tradition on which this palace was founded stretched back to the Ise shrine. This was a tradition based not on structural logic, but on esthetic appreciation. (The free-standing ridge supports, elongated principal rafters, and ridge crosslogs in the Ise shrine are by no means based on principles of dynamics.) It involved spatial divisions which in the middle ages developed into a kind of modular construction, but this latter, known as *kiwari,* was purely a matter of artistic balance rather than one of practicality and sound construction.

'The esthetic approach to structure was associated with the upper classes and with authority. It was displayed, for example, in the shoin-style mansions built by the dominant warrior class. Curiously, however, the principles of *kiwari* are not to be found in the Katsura Palace. Indeed, in so far as *kiwari* was a sign of authority, it was denied by the builders of the palace. Here one finds a new freedom, a new energy, which I believe to have come from the lower Japanese classes, the peasants and merchants who were forced to deal not with esthetic balance, but with actualities . . . The Katsura Palace in many ways flouts the tradition that preceded it and there are reasons to suppose that this flouting was deliberate.

'It is equally important to notice, however, that the longing for freedom expressed in Katsura was later repressed, so that in the long run it found an outlet only in the studiedly simple architectural styles associated with the tea ceremony and in the cramped seventeen-syllable poem.

'Until very recently, Japan was constantly under the control of an absolute state and the cultural energy of the people as a whole—energy with which they might have created new forms—was confined and suppressed. This was especially true in the Tokugawa period, when the government strove relentlessly to prevent social change. Only in our own times has the energy of which I speak begun to be released. It is still working in a confused medium and much remains to be done before real order is achieved, but

12 In an article accompanying the presentation of the Kagawa Prefectural Hall published in the review *The Japan Architect,* January–February, 1959.

it is certain that this energy will do much to convert Japanese tradition into something new and creative.

'It was with this thought in mind that I worked on the design for the Kagawa Prefectural Office. Whether I have succeeded in making something new of tradition, I cannot say, but I have tried.'

Fig. 21 Kurashiki is a town steeped in tradition. It has old houses with plastered and brick walls, of the type used for stores in the pre-modern period, and all this constitutes an unusual town-planning environment. But the old town faces a new development, through the creation of an industrial area, and this situation makes the town typical of modern industrial Japan. To design a City Hall, a Citizens' Square, an auditorium, for a town that faces such re-adjustment–these are challenging tasks.

'I believe,' Tange asserts,[13] 'that we Japanese architects have considered Japanese tradition from about every possible angle. The conclusion I have reached is that tradition is like a catalyst; it can stimulate or hasten creative activity, but not a trace of it remains in the finished product. The white plaster walls and the beautiful tradition of Kurashiki[14] were an inspiration for me and my team, but we made every effort to avoid any trace of them in our building. The fact that the building nevertheless is reminiscent of old Japanese warehouses in the log-cabin style was not anticipated. It only shows that we are still in the process of crystallisation.

'In a city of the scale of Kurashiki a new city hall can determine the direction of future growth, not merely for a short cycle, but for a long one. For this reason, it is better not to follow the past, but to create a new order.
Pl. 27, Fig. 21 I strongly hope that this city hall and auditorium will stimulate the re-development of Kurashiki.'

'The City Hall faces a Citizens' Square that is now nearing completion, and the complex as a whole was designed to have what I call a mass-human scale. With that in mind, I chose a structure of steel and concrete, which stresses the fact that this is a contemporary building. Other materials–those which have been commercialised and which as factory-produced materials are always changed after increasingly short periods of time–shorter cycles–betray their date because each year's model is different, but they do not give the building the stamp of its period.

'The mass-human scale is shown by a structure that has a long-term cycle. We first considered possibilities for the major structure, which determines the system of the whole building. Taking as basic two structural cores which enclose the central facilities and the vertical lines of traffic, we added to this a structure with a span of twenty metres.

'It was, however, no simple matter to associate this scale with the level of individual human scale. Consequently, we thought of a minor structure of precast concrete block and after many trials composed a single form and

13 *A Building and a Project,* presentation accompanying the publication of the plans for the Kurashiki City Hall in *The Japan Architect,* October, 1960.
14 In 1960 Kenzo Tange completed the Kurashiki City Hall, the first element in a re-organisation of the city centre, set in the general overall plan worked out by the architects, Kishida and Tayakama, which envisages the redevelopment of a wide area on the periphery and the conservation of the existing historical structure. The insertion of the new structure in the old surroundings is achieved with a brutal frankness, both in the design of the whole administrative centre and in the treatment of the single units, as if to emphasise the absolute incompatibility of a modern and democratic way of life with the old political and social system, whose crowded and tightly knit form is represented in the old town surrounding the building, composed of traditional Japanese single-family houses. Thus the first contrast which Tange suggests through this work is by nature a dimensional one. Once the whole plan is completed, the profile of the town will be dominated by the two great volumes of the City Hall and the Auditorium, standing in a great space with no reference to the city around, and will be a permanent reminder to all to consider their status as citizens and as Japanese, and to choose between a modern way of life and a traditional pattern.
The violence of the expression is thus a direct consequence of an attitude that finds a satisfactory and coherent architectural form, to an extent that is most unusual in European or American examples, apart from the work of Le Corbusier. Here the figurative force and the ideological message come so much together that the architecture may be termed 'epic'–it seeks to 'force a decision rather than allow for emotion'. Since Tange has chosen the path of violence, he pursues it to the extreme. His every interest is dominated by the theme he wants to express; simplicity is essential and Tange shapes his buildings in forms outstanding for their ostentatious geometrical simplicity (the City Hall is based on a parallelepiped, and the Auditorium on a truncated parallelepiped). The relationship between the two is achieved through the great square which physically links them and which endows them with the weight of two great *objets trouvés*. (Manfredo Tafuri, *op. cit.*)

7, 8. Plan for a Palace of the Arts (Kenzo Tange's graduating thesis), 1938

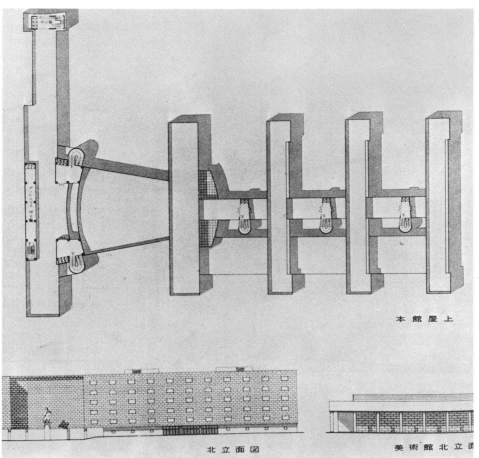

本館屋上

北立面図 美術館北立面

9. Plan for the Daitoa Kensetsu Memorial, 1942

space. I regret that we were unable here to develop the full structural meaning of this minor structure. If also it does not satisfy the full requirements of the human scales, it is because we wished, by establishing a scale of sequences, to consider the establishment of spatial flow from the plaza to the city hall and into the interior, and in a broader sense, the hierarchy of urban space, that is to say, of the space including the city hall, the plaza and the surrounding houses.'

Pls. 23, 24

Tange shows himself here to be perfectly aware of the limitations of buildings; he also sees them as exceptional vehicles for the transformation of a culture that is faced with the need for new communal symbols. Their imposing appearance is justified on the grounds of the need to underline the significance of the democratic process and the offices which the buildings house, without descending anywhere to mere rhetoric.

Apart from this, despite its monumental scale, the flexibility of the interior space – here we already find a modular arrangement – the unit between interior and exterior, the use of structural elements to expressive ends, the subtle vocabulary of technological forms – all qualities that had a place in traditional Japanese architecture – seem to point the way once again to the relationships between form and function, between the structure and expression, between the programme and proportion, confirming the authenticity of the designs of these buildings.

There are, however, less acceptable elements in the Kagawa Prefectural Office, that seem to look back to the building forms of pagodas, even though the organic joints of the ancient wooden structures are here translated into the undeniable elegance of concrete forms.[15] But the choice of such features was determined by the need to create buildings that would be immediately comprehensible to even the most unprepared levels of society.

Pl. 15
Fig. 5

Tange once said: 'Immediately after the Second World War and up to the 1950s, Japan struggled to rebuild and to restore its shattered economic life. The Japanese turned their eyes backwards, towards past traditions. In this climate of opinion, Japanese architects felt that they would not be in tune with popular feeling unless their designs followed the old traditions.'

Pls. 13, 15, 28, 44

The hierarchical division of a design on the basis of the cyclical nature of the individual parts, such as we find in the Kurashiki City Hall where it even comes to dominate the design on an expressive level, is exploited again and developed further, on the level of town-planning, in a theoretical project for a community of 25,000 people in Boston Bay, which Tange worked on with a group of students from the Massachusetts Institute of Technology in Cambridge, where he was invited for a year's professorship in 1959.

'There are many discrepancies between, on the one hand, the social phenomena and human environmental patterns being brought on by

Town-planning: the Boston project

Figs. 22–4

15 'Here again . . . we have reinforced concrete. While Le Corbusier leaves its function sometimes concealed, treating with anarchic flexibility the laws he himself laid down, this work by Kenzo Tange (the Kurashiki City Hall, in the 'Kenchiku Bunka' of September) seems a translation in cement of a wooden building. This impression is especially strong as regards the exterior of the building: the lines on the cement surface, the ends of the beams and the pilasters, the sequence of panelling . . . it seems as though a loving Japanese cabinet-maker scanned and shaped the modular parts, compressed the four sides of this symmetrical box with a refined flair for rhythmic composition. Now this play on the theme of wood in which the cornice and the base pillars (which are, on the other hand, unmistakable) make an unusual counterpoint, is most elegant but it is not vital. The plan does not represent an unusual solution, although it is satisfactory; but in the interior a great sense of space redeems it stereometrically and the whole is transformed by it; there is a fascinating play on the modulations of light and structure which are continually accentuated by the detail. But this is nevertheless all tradition. The effort Japan is making to endow reinforced concrete with that same vitality that belongs with her great architectural tradition is meritorious; but she must, at least for the present, avoid solutions of elegance; otherwise the antimony is fatal. . .' (in L'Architettura, No. 63, January, 1961, pp. 624–5). 'The Japanese architectural tradition is founded on techniques and materials that are antithetical to reinforced concrete. The structural framework could easily be transferred from wood to steel, and in that transition, the artistic configuration of lines and transparent panels did not undergo any radical alteration. But the qualities inherent in reinforced concrete are those of curved, flowing plastic form. To use reinforced concrete in columns and beams as if it was steel means sacrificing its genuine meaning.' (Bruno Zevi, 'Un giapponese contro la tradizione', in L'Espresso, 20th September, 1959, p. 16.)

10. Aerial view of the Doyotima district with the Dentsu Building, Osaka, 1957–60. The rapid changes in the urban environment invalidated Tange's original conception of the site: he envisaged the building overlooking the canal without the elevated motorways

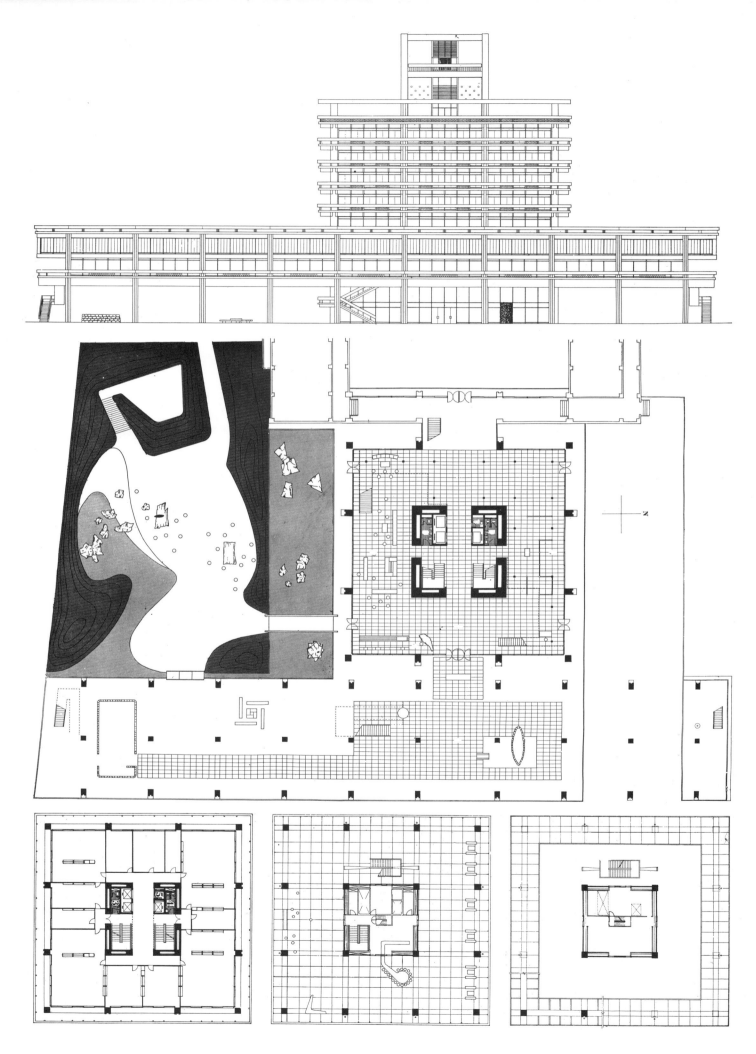

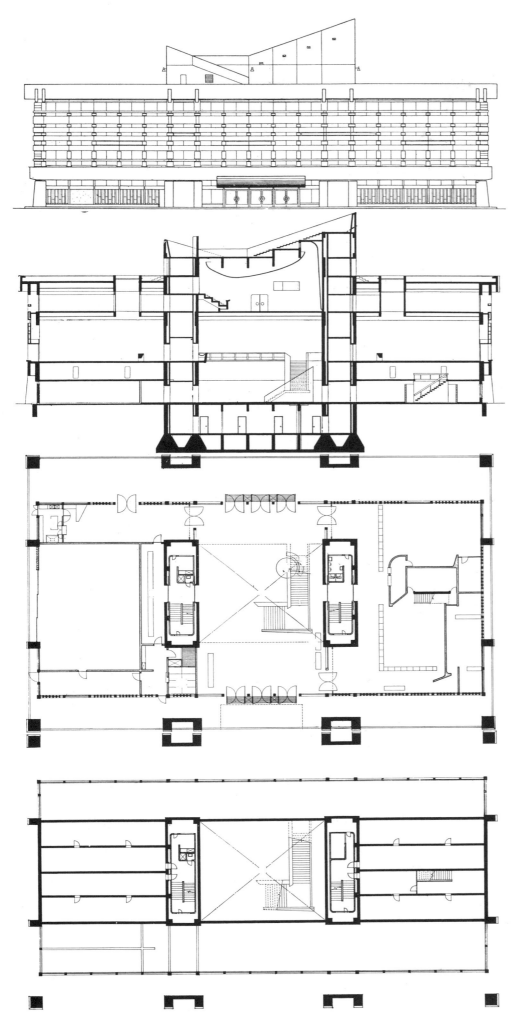

11–15. Kagawa Prefectural Office,
Takamatsu, 1955–8. Elevation,
ground floor, upper floors
and roof-level plans

16–19. City Hall, Kurashiki,
1957–60. Elevation,
ground floor plan,
plan of floors on upper levels

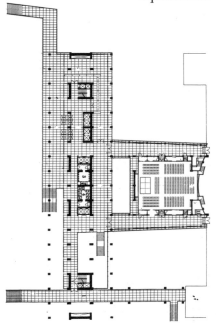

technological progress in the latter part of the twentieth century and, on the other, the natural desire for something more human. To overcome these discrepancies is the responsibility that falls on architects and city-planners. I think we must face up to this responsibility, which involves problems that cannot be solved with methods and terminology already in existence. In my opinion, we must create a new prototype.

'. . . The city must serve as a place to live, a place to work, a place to play, and a place for traffic involved in these three activities. The most important factor involved in making a city an organic entity is in all probability the core. After analysing the function and structure of the city, we come upon an even more important question which is that of a comprehensive method of linking the various functions. However, the house, the street, the district, the city–these various levels of the community are the elements which compose a city. Each type must have a certain degree of unity and perfection, and at the same time it must open on to the higher level and create a system for a larger entity. We must consider the problem of preserving identity at each level, and at the same time we must find some way of making the meaning and value of each element comprehensible within the total system.

'When it comes to the problem of a high degree of community life or of the method for linking the various functions of the city, modern means of transportation introduce new possibilities. The highway is on the way to deciding a new system of association, both visually and functionally, but the superhuman scale involved in a highway system lacks unity with existing architectural forms. This does not mean, of course, that the superhuman scale is therefore to be denied. Instead, we must consider an order which will link it with the human scale.

'Whereas the total system in cities is being defined by huge construction work, involving things like highways, over a long period of time, the dwelling unit is changing over a short period, and factory-produced elements over an even shorter one.

'Several questions occur. Can architecture not constitute a long-term structure which can define the system? With factory-produced elements, cannot houses which would be suitable to a shorter time-span be constructed? Is it not possible to find an order which will associate the two? Cannot we conceive of a major structure and a minor structure which, like the trunk and leaves of a tree, are linked, but which change according to different cycles? Can the major structures not have the same possibility for growth as a tree trunk?'

Of the seven projects produced by the students, only one exemplified Tange's ideas clearly. The proposal was worked on during the academic year by George Pillorge, Edward Haladay, Ted Niederman and Gustave Solomons.

Fig. 22

The project visualised two primary residential structures based on a continuous triangular section. Within these, streets lead off the motorways, and a mono-rail provides facilities for bulk transport. There are parking areas and elevators for vertical movement. Spatially, the plan is laid out to provide a lasting urban framework. The general arrangement provides a layout for human needs based on modern technological advances. The division of space follows a hierarchy of different levels. There is the scale provided by nature, the superhuman scale (of technology), the mass-human scale, and finally the scale of the individual human being in his daily existence. Within the triangular structure there are open spaces for community centres. These spaces have the capacity for functions on a mass scale, and they are illuminated by natural daylight through wide openings. At every third level (human scale) there are walkways, and along these, rows of single-family houses.

'The triangular major structure is to be thought of as man-made nature rather than man-made land, or as nature improved upon. It is rich in variety, as in nature, and it has an order which reflects the characteristics

of its period. The individual housing units attached to its surface form the minor structure and the forms of these may be left to individual choice. At this microscopic level, the details and the placing of the house can also be left to individual taste; the houses are elements which can change and grow freely according to short cycles, and they form the visual texture. The significance of these houses is that they permit the individual to identify himself within the system and make this identification comprehensible.'

The Boston Bay Project is a proposal which tries to focus a particular problem, but it glosses over some factors, such as the political and social system, the distribution of investment capital, the ownership of land and even the constructional systems.

Utopianism as political action

In 1958 the Japan Housing Company, in order to combat the problem of land speculation, put forward a proposal for the development of Tokyo Bay through a system of dams of the sort common in Holland.[16]

The subject has affinities with, among other things, the need architects have to break the anonymity which encircles their creations, to create a real relationship between the latter and the environment in which they are placed.

Two years later Tange took up this theme again, developing further on a local level the criteria which had already been applied to the Boston project, with a plan for the development of Tokyo into the bay that aroused immediate enthusiasm and once again placed its author at the forefront of international discussion on town-planning.

At the World Design Conference, held in Tokyo in May, 1960, Tange in a long address[17] explained the ideological and philosophical background to his proposal.

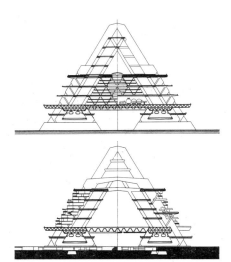

'As we leave the earlier half of the twentieth century and proceed into the second half, I have the feeling that we are experiencing vital changes in cultural forms, social structure and human environment. There is no way to predict the future, but I believe we can say this much: the current great change is resulting from the development of atomic energy and electronics and the direction of the change is not towards unregulated expansion of energy, but toward the controlling and planning of its development. Mankind is engaged in a second attempt to gain superiority over scientific techniques.

'The release of atomic energy has led us to discover such things as automatic brains to control its great power, and ultimately it has released a new consciousness of humanity . . . This new consciousness may have come in part through fear of the atomic bomb, but in a larger sense it results from the freeing of new energy. The more powerful scientific energy becomes, the stronger man's consciousness of his own existence will become.

'It must be recognised that scientific progress is one of the determining factors in our future, and that whatever man's desires or hopes, science itself can determine much. On the other hand, as science becomes social reality, it will doubtless be mankind which decides whether new discoveries

16 In the spring of 1958, Kyuro Kano, the president of the Japan Housing Corporation, made a proposal involving the filling in of the northern part of the bay, with the gain of a land area of 83,225 square metres; one and a half times the area at present within the bounds of the city. This proposal provoked a number of doubts regarding:
(1) the drastic nature of the change
(2) the fact that the space gained would be used to extend the urban and sprawl of the present Tokyo periphery.

Other plans were drawn up to make provision against this possibility. Masato Otaka, an architect with Kunio Mayekawa (and Associates), put forward the following solution: great piles are placed on the bed of the ocean in various appropriate parts of the bay and covered with concrete 'islands', for it would be absurd, as Otaka says, to fill up an area that later had to be excavated for the foundations of buildings. Half the cost of the entire operation would be saved if the land fill was done away with. The entire town would be placed on a series of slabs – Otaka even speaks of woods being placed on such slabs. Kikutake's proposal is for a floating town, a series of artificial islands connected by sea and air links. While these remain unrealisable dreams – Kikutake himself admits as much – he also says that there should be nothing in a space age of the future to prevent such solutions (in *The Japan Architect*, May, 1959).
17 Later published in *The Japan Architect*, October, 1960, under the title *Technology and Humanity*.

22–4. Plan for a community of 25,000 people in Boston Bay, 1960. Elevation and model

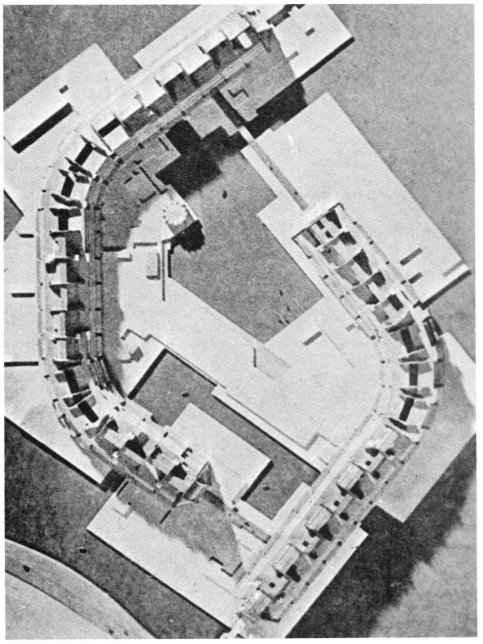

25. Project entered for the international competition for the World Health Organisation building in Geneva, 1960

26. Proposal for the extension of Tokyo into the Bay, 1961. Plan

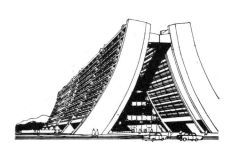

are beneficial or harmful to man and whether they are to be accepted or rejected.

'. . . I like to think that there is something deep in our own world of reality that will create a dynamic balance between technology and human existence, for this relationship has a decisive effect on contemporary cultural forms and social structure. I do not mean to say, however, that I regard technology as humanity's servant or an extension of man's hand. I am by no means that optimistic; on the contrary, when I consider the social phenomena that have been brought on by technological development, I am forced to conclude that while technology progresses in some ways, in others it tends to separate itself more and more from humanity. There is no need to adopt the fatalistic idea that mankind is a fixed historical entity and that progress must inevitably deepen the rift between technology and humanity. I believe we must seek out the unbalanced features of the reality that surrounds us and overcome them, find the problems we must solve and challenge them. Without this challenge, creative energy will not manifest itself, and only creativeness can bridge the gap. Indeed, creativeness *is* bridging the gap.

'Architects and designers are the only people who stand in the middle ground between technology and humanity and it is therefore essential that with the advance of science they manifest more and more creativeness. In this age of change, the designs and architectural ideals of the first half of the twentieth century are no longer sufficient solutions for the problems that are growing in scope every day. They are simply not suitable to the age. The time has come for design to be revolutionised from within.

'Let us concentrate for a moment on man's human environment. What problems does it actually present? In my opinion, the first is the problem of mobility, which is gradually becoming more widespread and more rapid. With regard to distance, mobility is a question of conquering distance. This is a matter of speed and scale. Man himself walks, as he has always walked, in steps of less than one meter each, but at the same time speeds of 100 kilometers per hour or more are part of our everyday life. Mobility considered as a complex of scale and speed, is, in fact, a problem involving just plain man with a branch of technology that is in the process of rapid development. Present-day Tokyo is a huge, growling conglomeration of pedestrians, bicycles, automobiles, trucks and streetcars. On almost any downtown street there is a wild confusion of pedestrians and automobiles snarling at each other like the natural enemies that they are. A natural human scale exists in the same space with a superhuman scale created by technology and there is nothing to bring harmony between them and to unify them. This applies not only in the functional sense, but in the visual sense.

'With respect to the problem of scale, I have been considering what I call a mass-human scale. This is a standard needed when human beings act as groups and masses rather than as individuals. Excellent examples are to be found in European town squares, city halls, and churches of the middle ages, where there is an order that harmonises the human scale with the mass-human scale. In considering our modern cities, I believe that we must look for an order which will have the same effect, and which at the same time will bring the superhuman scale into harmony with the human scale.

'With regard to time, mobility is a problem of change and growth.[18] Rapidly advancing technology is increasing the speed at which our social life expands and changes. Under the influence of commercialism, such things as our everyday necessities and the style of automobiles change every year . . . Even our dwellings cease to be serviceable after five or ten years. Short-lived items are becoming more and more short-lived and the cycle of change is shrinking at a corresponding rate.

'On the other hand, the accumulation of capital has made it possible to build in large-scale operations. Reformations of natural topography, dams,

27, 28. Proposal for the extension
of Tokyo into the Bay.
Detail of the main axis,
in elevation, plan, model

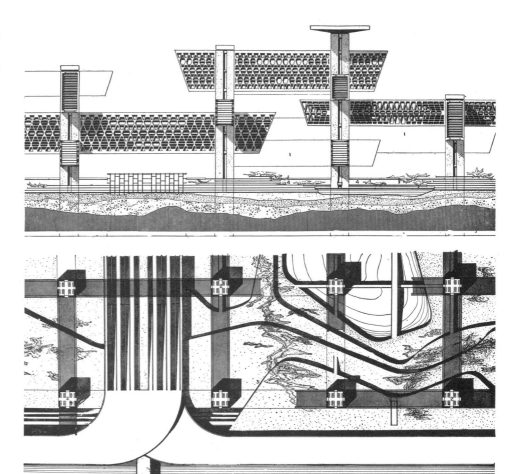

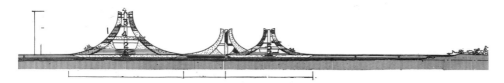

29, 30. Proposal for the extension of Tokyo into the Bay. Detail of the residential area with housing units, in elevation, plan, model

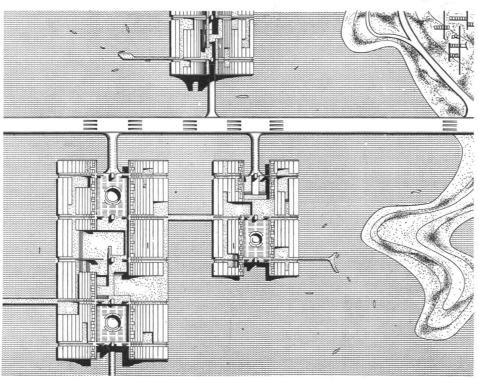

31. Aerial view of the Olympic
buildings at Harajuku, Tokyo.
1961–4

harbours, and highways are of a size and scope that involve long cycles of time, and these are the man-made works that tend to decide the overall system of the age.

'The two tendencies—toward shorter cycles and toward longer cycles—are both necessary to modern life and humanity itself. Life, or for that matter any organism, is composed of elements that change and elements that do not change; the cells of the body renew themselves, but the body itself remains stable. In our cities there are changing fashions and unchanging elements that determine the character of the age. The time has come, I think, when we must find ways of overcoming the discrepancies between these two. The problem has emerged in our society as one of mobility.

'The second great problem that I would like to consider is that of the influence of mass communication and mass production in our lives. Like material things, we human beings are becoming at once more universal and more anonymous . . . It is often difficult to tell whether a building is a hospital or a church. People, too, are becoming more alike throughout the world and are being organised into huge groups in which they become anonymous. The desire for individuality, however, seems to be basic to human nature and one result is the prevalence of ridiculous advertisements in which people seek to identify themselves. To summarise, there are conflicting trends toward universality and individuality, toward anonymity and identification. These form one of the great cultural dilemmas of our time. In Tokyo, for example, almost every district has approximately the same population density and buildings of the same height. They are all similar in function and they are all growing in the same shoddy way. . . .

'We live in a world where great incompatibles co-exist: the human scale and the superhuman scale, stability and mobility, permanence and change, identity and anonymity, comprehensibility and universality. These are reflections of the gap between advancing technology and static humanity with its historical existence. How can the gap be spanned? How can order be imposed on confusion? The only answer is human ingenuity, as I have already said, but it should be added that no amount of ingenuity can create without method.

'When it comes to method, I believe that we can take a hint from the various approaches in the modern sciences. One science is the study of life; the other, that of physics or mathematics. The principle of life has not yet been discovered, but organisms can be viewed macroscopically as stable structures composed of orderly arrangements of cells. The organism lives, however, because of the constant metabolism of the cells, and this must be examined microscopically. Atoms and electrons, too, must be observed on this scale, but when observation of them reveals free, haphazard movement, the scientist or the mathematician develops group theories or theories of probability.

'The function of science, then, is to approach things both macroscopically and microscopically. The movement of life is not viewed as having no order, even though we do not know the real nature of life . . . The problem is the basic one of order versus freedom, and style versus spontaneity, but

18 'Tange speaks of an urban spatial arrangement that is ultimately fluid, open and democratic, but that which he gives us is in fact so rigid and systematic as to be unrealisable in a free society. He affirms that the direction of the civic axis is variable, and it need not necessarily extend into the bay; but once the choice has been made, it is difficult to make it flexible without dispensing with the final limits of the plan altogether.

Tange answers these objections as follows: "We must plan in advance. If we rely on spontaneous urban growth, we stand on the threshold of a catastrophe." He is right, but he does not notice that his plan only adds a further chapter to the long list of nineteenth-century utopian exercises.' (Bruno Zevi, 'Costruiranno la capitale sulle palafitte—Piano regolatore per Tokyo', *L'Espresso*, 4th March, 1962, p. 19.)

'We can at this point make a brief note of the substantial affinity between Tange's attitude and that of Le Corbusier, in his address to the CIAM in Brussels in 1930 on the problems facing cities, when he spoke of the authority that must emerge from the technical solutions that would be developed. This is an authority that the modern movement has waited for in vain. And both the contemporary projects of Le Corbusier (notably the plans for Algiers and Buenos Aires) and those of Tange attempt the creation of such an authority in the resolution of the whole range of problems in a "single architectural theme".' (Manfredo Tafuri, *op. cit.*)

the important thing is that only by approaching both extremes can we arrive at the true picture of the whole. To side with one is not enough. The task is to create order within what appears to be incompatibility.'

Figs. 26–30 The attempted combination of these different requirements is obvious in Tange's Tokyo Bay plan, but the results do not go beyond the limits of an ideal city conception, even though the most detailed reasoning and economic calculations would have us believe otherwise. Although the forms adopted in the plan are exciting, they are not new to contemporary architecture. In spite of this, their restatement in the delicate and sensitive Japanese idiom endows their reality with a new dimension.

The new scale of social relations is modelled on a city which develops along a linear axis, of which the limitations were already well-known to Western town-planners. Nor does Tange's plan possess either the organic of the extreme capacity for adaptation of the traditional Japanese town, which some of the utopian planners in 1960 wished to preserve. The value of the project consisted in the reactions which it provoked, and in its expression of the 'precise desire to maintain intact the values of the town by working on the friction points that have developed'.[19]

The work of the 1960 planners was thus more important for the stimulus which it gave, rather than for any practical possibility of its realisation in fact. Japanese architects face unprecedented opportunities and the phenomenal capacity of the construction industry in Japan is demonstrated by the building of the Tokaido railway, or the incredible speed with which Tokyo's motorways were erected. The funds allocated for the next thirty years amount to the staggering figure of 175 trillion dollars. Nevertheless, within the current political situation it is impossible, precisely on account of the division of interests where they should be united, to visualise a form of politics with a broader approach.

Against this background it is easy to see the importance of the role of the architect as a promoter of utopian ideals, since these are the formal incarnation of a precise moment in a wider revolutionary movement that encompasses the whole social and technological framework.

Architecture as a symbol

The interest which the plan provoked did not however succeed in promoting political involvement in town-planning. And the projects which Tange completed during these years are isolated structures, with no possibility of any link with the environment in which they are situated, with which they are sometimes in open contrast. The contrast in scale reaches dramatic Pls. 42–5 proportions in the Sports Centre attached to the Kagawa Prefectural Office, built in 1964. Tange's buildings were by this time endowed with much greater expressive freedom.

Pls. 29, 30 For Rikkyo University Tange built (1961) a library, in red brick so as not to clash with the Neogothic buildings on the campus. The hills of Totsuka offered a similar opportunity as for Le Corbusier at Ronchamp for Pl. 31 Tange to endow the Golf Club building (1961) with notably plastic form. This accords well with the curvilinear forms of the slopes, but this sculptural liberty impinges upon the compositional severity.[20] The bold forms of the Cultural Centre at Nichinan (1962) achieve a dialogue with the rocky landscape.[21] The bareness of the concrete, the absence of any features

19 G. Grassi, 'La citta come prestazione vitale', in *Casabella-Continuità*, No. 258, December, 1961.
20 *The Architectural Review* described this building as 'Tange at his most sculptural'.

'The design of the building is most rich in imaginative forms; to be fully appreciated, it should be seen as a work of sculpture. As such it is most successful, although as a building it is perhaps less successful. The greater part of the clubhouse is roofed by an inverted shell, supported by six (three to the north and three to the south) massive and dramatic pillars. Underneath the roof the side panels are of glass and aluminium.' (From the editorial of *The Japan Architect* of January, 1963.)
21 'Tange's latest work (the Nichinan Cultural Centre) is indubitably his most violent. Here the visible reinforced concrete is moulded and treated as a tortured surface, pierced here and there by openings, that contrast with a few misshapen excrescences, bringing the play of volumes close to that "abstract" expressiveness (the critic Yuichiro Kojiro compared these surfaces to the accidental effects of erosion) that is taken up again in the interior of the Auditorium. Here the curtain painted by Toko Shimada in an 'action-painting' technique catches precisely the mood of Tange's emphatic space.' (Manfredo Tafuri, *op. cit.*)

arbitrarily derived from the common architectural vocabulary, link the building organically with its environment.

For the Olympic Games in 1964 Tange built in the centre of Tokyo the National Gymnasium, comprising a great covered stadium with a seating capacity of 15,000 around a number of swimming pools (the space can be transformed into an ice-rink) and a smaller stadium with 4,000 seats, which can be used for various purposes. The connecting building, which is partly underground, includes the administrative offices, a restaurant and a covered promenade.

Pls. 32–41
Fig. 31

These buildings are intrinsically attractive and have among the most beautiful of all modern designs. The Japanese tradition of figurative elegance almost causes the subtle play of forms here to go beyond the limits of abstraction. Nevertheless, Tange follows the pattern of his inspiration with a profound awareness of the structural possibilities.

One of the fundamental problems was the choice of a structure to cover the vast area of the stadium. Tange selected a tensile structure in steel. 'By comparison with the convex space of a dome, the concave figuration of a suspension structure encloses a great deal less space and lightens heating and air conditioning loads and makes acoustic control easier.

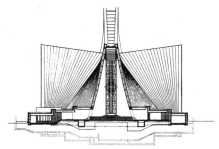

32. St Mary's Roman Catholic Cathedral, Tokyo. Elevation

'What made me personally decide on this structural method, however, was the possibility I saw in it of creating an "open form". From the outset, the structural form aside, we felt the need for openness to greet and see of vast numbers of people, but we also felt that this openness must not be merely a matter of hydrodynamic functions, but should also have a psychological meaning. Speaking conversely, we wanted to eliminate the feeling of enclosure by the roof and the closed-in stands. We also gave consideration to the need for an open form in order to have a visual and physical connection between the main gymnasium and the gymnasium annex in the event of other buildings being added to the group in the future.

'The principal axes of the main gymnasium are cables suspended, much as in a bridge, between two huge pillars. The back stays on either end of the building are anchored for stability. On either side of the cable are half-moon inclined stands. The upper, sloping parts of these stands, while forming the spectators' main sight line, also describe arching slopes in space that function structurally as vast inclined arches. The roof is suspended between the axial cable and the upper edges of the stands and is formed of a great many suspended steel branch cables. A spindle-shaped opening can be made between the tensile force of the branches by means of axial cables. These openings will later serve as top-lighting. The line of reactional force of the stands sweeps along the upper arches and arrives at the base points of the large columns where both of the two vast arches achieve a state of equilibrium. The concave line of the cable and the convex lines of the upper edges of the stands form double curved planes that have a negative relationship and which stabilise the curved surfaces of the building . . . The form feeling of the catenary, which comes from the suspension structure, is a keynote for the steel roof structure; but to make the tensile structure possible, the compression of the base part is necessary. The arch then becomes the keynote for the concrete structure.'

The co-ordination of such a structure with extremely precise spatial and functional requirements was extremely difficult, as it was, also, to maintain a unity of scale with elements of such vastly differing size. Nevertheless the formal unity that is essential to a work of this sort was maintained and fully achieved.

The only reservations are of a town-planning nature. Built on an area of ground that is too limited even in a functional sense (there is insufficient parking space and not enough room for pedestrian access), the stadiums appear to float like magic boats in the midst of the disorder of the town which surrounds them.

In 1965 Tange built the Roman Catholic Cathedral of St Mary in Tokyo. This has an attractive design although its functional interpretation has led

Pls. 46–50
Fig. 32

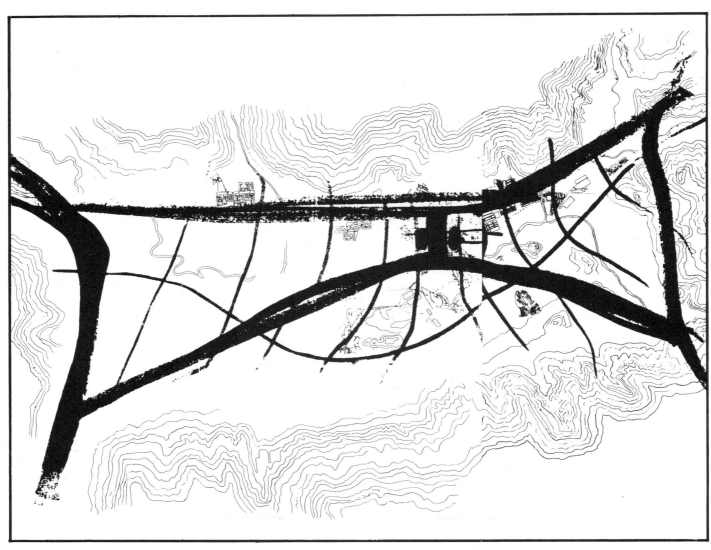

33, 34. Plan for the reconstruction of Skopje, 1965–6. Sketch of the main plan, detail of the model with the City Gate

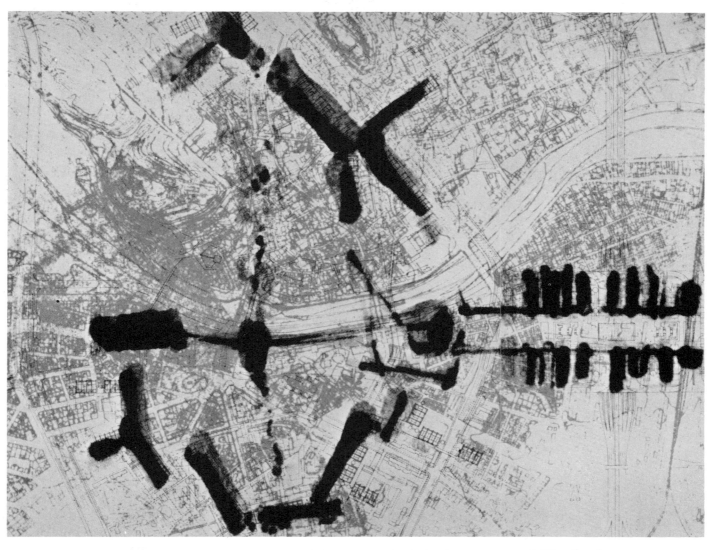

35, 36. Plan for the
reconstruction of Skopje. Sketch
of the main elements in the plan,
detail of the model with
the shopping centre

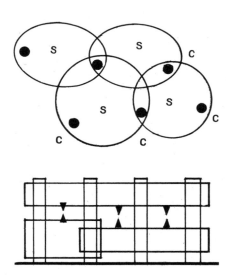

Architecture and town-planning co-ordinated: the Skopje plan

Pls. 60–3
Figs. 33–6

to perhaps excessively abstract ends. Ultimately, however, the design is based on extremely free and elegant curves (like those of medieval bastions or samurai swords) which meet at the top in a symbolic cross.

Nevertheless the materials used do not appear to be the most suitable for such forms. (Perhaps the model that ought to have been looked at in this connection was Le Corbusier's Philips Pavilion, or indeed the Olympic stadiums, where the cement wall is replaced by a more organic structure supported by steel cables.) Another unsatisfactory element is the junction of the structure with the ground level, which lacks continuity, and the small spaces at the base are out of tune with the elegant sweep of the upper part.

In these works, Tange freed himself completely from references to tradition and reached that state of creativity which he mentioned in the project for Kurashiki. Here tradition is no shackle, but rather it represents the freedom to be oneself, with perfect accord between the forms and that which generated them.

In 1966 Tange won the competition for the reconstruction of the town of Skopje (Yugoslavia) which had been destroyed by an earthquake, with a design that was a notable contribution to modern town-planning (although considered too expensive to carry through).[22] The project represents a synthesis of his previous experience; we find an embodiment in a clear and coherent fashion of the town-planning notion that free communication between the separate parts should be the core and symbol of the modern town, just as the cathedral had been in the middle ages. This idea is expressed, in the Skopje plan, in the perfect co-ordination of the road system with the architectural. The system represented a sophistication of ideas already present in the Tokyo Bay plan, where they appeared for the first time.

The primary concept that Tange adopts as his solution is founded on the linear development of communication, starting from the largest structure and culminating in the central axes. The latter are the starting-points for the complex spatial structures that form the nucleus of the smaller city centre. The 'walls' are identified in the towers which house the stairs and elevators.

The most interesting part of the plan is the so-called 'City-Gate' which is above the railway station and on the axis of the centre. The whole plan is permeated by a combination of architecture and town-planning, worked on like a complex mechanism, so that the resulting spatial solution is extremely satisfactory. Just as in the plans for Boston and Tokyo, the local environment determines the function and the forms adopted. The commercial plaza is especially attractive.

The arrangements for traffic in the zone that is deliberately monumental are akin to the backbone of the Tokyo plan: the zone becomes the starting-point for branches, which like the branches of a tree, progress in an organic fashion determined by the lie of the land and the survival of some of the old buildings of Skopje.[23]

22 'From those who participated in the international competition, which closed on the 20th July, 1965, the following groups were invited: Kenzo Tange (Japan), Van den Broek and Bakema (Holland), L. Piccinato (Italy), M. Rotival (USA), A. Djordjevic (Yugoslavia), E. Ravnikar (Yugoslavia), R. Miscevic (Yugoslavia), S. Brezoski (Yugoslavia). The winner was Tange, and Miscevic came second. It is worthwhile taking note of what the jury had to say, and commenting on Tange's participation in the competition. The jury adjudged Miscevic's plan "mean in its proposals but nevertheless worthy of second prize because it could be carried out in stages and without difficulty". Needless to say, it was Miscevic's plan that would be carried out, with a few modifications.

'In this situation one is prompted to say two things—in the first place there were other projects that could be undertaken with little difficulty, for instance those of Djordjevic and Piccinato, that were less mean in the proposals they offered; in the second place it is clear that Tange's first prize is an ambiguous award. Tange advanced a project that was far beyond the current limited means available in Yugoslavia, so the jury awarded the first prize to a plan which they could not use.

'This not a positive attitude, and it is indicative of some confused thinking. Nor is it clear whether Tange, who had been invited to resolve a particular problem, produced a work that was useless so far as the client was concerned.

'In this it is not intended to see Tange's work as useless, nor to diminish its obvious merit; indeed one must underline the importance of work such as that which Tange undertook and urge that this sort of work should be financed by an international body.' (L. M. Boschini, 'Il concorso per il centro di Skopje', in Casabella, No. 307, 1966.)

37, 38. Communications Centre for the Yamanashi Region, Kofu, 1966–7. Diagram illustrating the spatial layout (S = Space, C = Core element)

39–43. Communications Centre for the Yamanashi Region, Kofu. Elevation and plans

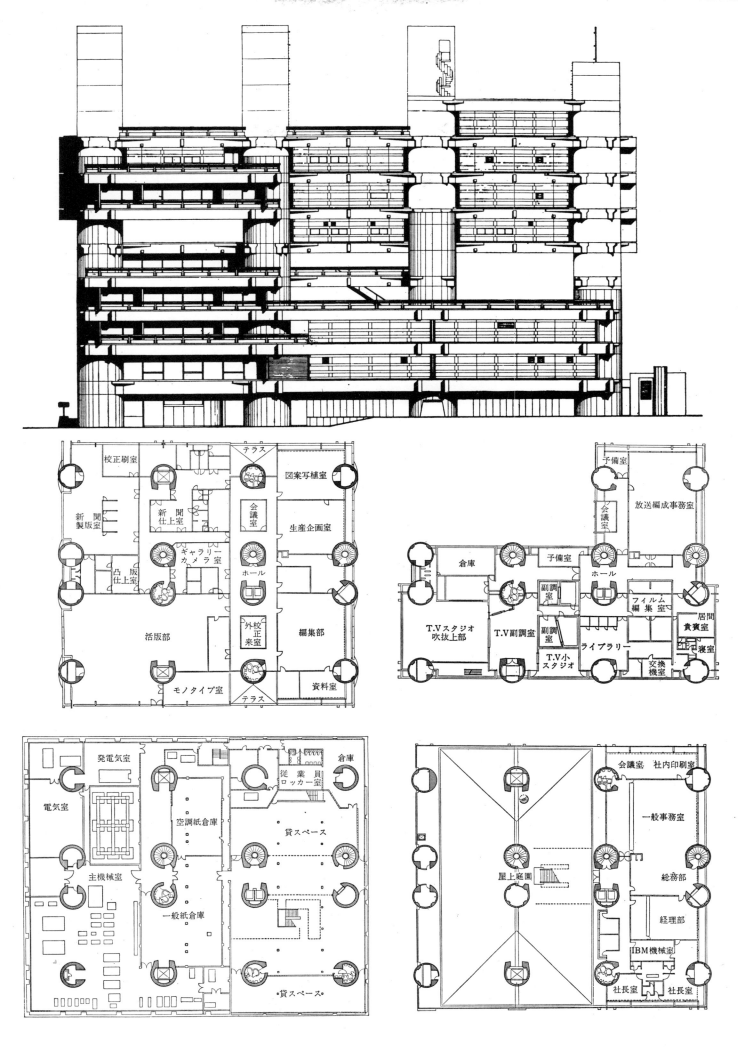

校正刷室
新聞製版室
新聞仕上室
凸版仕上室
ギャラリーカメラ室
テラス
会議室
ホール
外校正来室
活版部
モノタイプ室
テラス
図案写植室
生産企画室
編集部
資料室

予備室
会議室
放送編成事務室
倉庫
予備室
副調室
ホール
T.Vスタジオ吹抜上部
T.V副調室
副調室
T.V小スタジオ
ライブラリー
フィルム編集室
居間
貴賓室
寝室
交換機室

発電気室
電気室
空調紙倉庫
従業員ロッカー室
倉庫
貸スペース
主機械室
一般紙倉庫
貸スペース

会議室　社内印刷室
一般事務室
屋上庭園
総務部
経理部
IBM機械室
社長室　社長室

'The large buildings connected with the roads are very interesting. The large triangular forms that were a characteristic of the Boston and Tokyo plans, but which were perhaps too imposing and only justifiable if the plan was being worked out on water, are abandoned. A spatial system carried on immense self-supporting wall-beams stems from enormous supporting columns which also house the services. This is certainly a more practical and more practicable approach. It provides hope for a possible real solution to the dramatic problems of the modern town.'[24]

Communications as the basis of spatial structure

Pls. 57–9
Figs. 44, 45, 47

Two years later Tange published the plan for Skopje in the reviews *Shinkenchiky, Kenkikubunka* and *The Japan Architect* (or rather a revised and more detailed version of the plan which had won the international competition in 1965), together with the plans for the Head Office of the Dentsu Advertising Company, intended as the first stage in the redevelopment of the Tsukiji[25] area in Tokyo, and for the Communications Centre of the Yamanashi region which was built at Kofu in 1967.[26]

The three projects, which belong to the same phase of Tange's work that began with the Tokyo Plan of 1960, offer a new approach to the problems of a high density urban environment. The architect introduced them in a critical account which also provided the opportunity for a retrospective examination in terms of the point of development he had then reached and his now more demanding standards.

'Looking back over my attitude toward architecture and urban design, I find that my earliest approach was a functional one but that very soon problems of surpassing the boundaries of functionalism emerged. I had already begun to think of interior and exterior functions in the Hiroshima plan and to consider ways of making exterior spaces and social spaces correspond to exterior function. The same was true of the Tokyo City Hall and the Kagawa Prefectural Hall.

'Within the limits of the functional approach, to ensure a typified correspondence between function and space, not only must the function itself be identified but so must the corresponding space. The process of arriving at such a correspondence was one of the main characteristics of our functional approach. Materialising this relationship is a part of materialising the interior functional relationship between aim and means. If we call this framework a functional unit, we find that it is one of the elements in the make-up of a city. Within this functional unit we find that space and form give typified expression to the individual identities of the functions. We were to some extent giving conscious application to this idea in the Nichinan Culture

23 'In spite of its visionary boldness, Tange's plan adheres more closely than those of the other competitors to the old regulations, although he breathes new life into them. In the first place he succeeded in providing a satisfactory integration of the hill, the old Kale fortress and the various nuclei of old buildings that survived; the monumental link which he envisaged with the old reconstructed square near the Dusan bridge is particularly interesting. We may conclude by saying that Tange's plan has its principal virtue in the sublimation of the avant-garde ideas that have their real place in the future development of society. The dream-world of the first modern visionaries, from Sant'Elia to Friedman, finds real and material form here. It is incumbent on us to make that world a reality.' (M. Mitrovic, 'La eliopolis di Tange', in *Casabella*, No. 307, 1966.)

24 M. Mitrovic, 'Il concorso per il centro di Skopje', *Casabella*, No. 307, July, 1966.

25 The failure to carry out the first design for the Head Office of the Dentsu Company in Tokyo represents one of the major lost opportunities in modern architecture. Conceived as a part of the redevelopment of the Tsukiji quarter in Tokyo, it constituted a first step in the materialisation of the 1960 Plan for Tokyo. Yoshida, the last president of the Dentsu Co., wanted a building that should symbolise the activity of his own company, and found Tange's plan, which followed closely the theory of the flow of communications, absolutely consistent with the unrhetorical approach he had in mind. The new law controlling the height of buildings had just come into force and would have enabled the building–unlike the Communications Centre at Kofu–to reach an appropriate height.

But the Japanese economy took an unfavourable turn, and this coincided with the death of the old president of the company, and his successors cut the budget for the building by 60%. So Tange hurriedly produced a quite different second version, which lacks the incision of the first and smacks of compromise, even though the structural arrangement of the load-bearing wall is interesting as a technical novelty.

26 '"The way in which Kenzo Tange has reconciled the individual role of the architect with the needs of society is typical of him and of our society," writes Terence Farrel in the RIBA Journal of February, 1969. This is an opinion which we can share, at least in the sense of a "utopia" in which there is an awareness of technical feasibilities.' (Bruno Zevi, in *L'Architettura* XI, 1967.)

Hall and in the Takamatsu Housing Development.

'When the functional content accompanies a metaphysical feature, however, individual expression is sometimes bathed in the symbolic. We consciously employed this type of expression to some extent in the National Indoor Stadium and in the Tokyo St Mary's Cathedral.

'We used a spatial system with columns, which we called *pilotis,* external function, or social spaces, to provide relationships between the functional unit that is an element in the city and the other city elements.

'If we proceed to generalise even further, we run up against problems that seem impossible to solve with the functional approach alone. We find that in addition to "functioning", we also need to give spaces structure. We came to believe that developing the process of "structuring" is the basic theme of urban design.

'As we have mentioned, the urban design method involves both the process of giving function and that of giving structure to spaces. When we give a typified form to a typified function, that function is immediately apparent to the eye and has an identity of its own. If we pursue this notion further, we see that we can express through form not only a space's physical function, but its metaphysical one as well. At this stage, when a certain space gives symbolic expression to its function, we require a symbolic approach.

'Actually the process of giving structure to the space contains within itself a symbolic way of thinking. Giving symbolic significance to the operation of structuring is useful in developing a design inwards and in having people understand the design.

'We made ample use of this attitude at Skopje. For instance, in applying the name "City Gate", we not only gave ourselves the hint that we should use something physically gate-like in this area, but we also planted in the minds of the people the understanding that this is the gate through which one enters the town of Skopje. If the design is false to the name, the citizens will reject it.

'The City Wall, too, gained fame, and even though at one point the opinion emerged that perhaps the Wall was an obstacle that we should abandon, the people of the city were opposed to do away with it. They understand a city wall and it became the centre of our image of what symbolises the city. Now we are told that we definitely should not abandon the Wall.[27]

'We have learnt through experience that it is necessary for a variety of symbolic process to emerge during the operation of structuring.

Figs. 34, 36

'While working on our plan, we had to remember that the full meaning of an urban design does not emerge from the paper plan, but only when it is tried in three-dimensional form. It was therefore necessary to work our plan to quite small detail and anticipate the architectural forms that would be employed. If it had been possible, it would have been useful to make detailed architectural studies of the centre.

'Indeed to proceed directly from an overall urban study to individual buildings is never good practice. I also think that to build extensive complexes is economically more favourable than investing in small unitary constructions.

'We decided then to work out a detailed urban plan to the architectural details level. In this third phase of planning we divided the whole project

27 'Kenzo Tange has won the international competition for the reconstruction of the Yugoslav town of Skopje. Looking at his plan, it would be impossible to give it a wholly negative judgement. Harking back to the concepts of "metabolism" and "metamorphosis", one must distinguish between an idea of urban design in which spontaneous development and change is envisaged, and the opposite criterion on which Tange founds his work. For an organic development of a town, five conditions have to be present: lightness, flexibility, natural simplicity, incompleteness and elegance. But Tange weighs Skopje down with heavy, rigid, intellectually schematic and disproportionate designs. But do not misunderstand; the question is not one merely to do with dimensions, for one can have a skyscraper that is refined, flexible, light, "incomplete" and a small house that is massive, inelastic, out of proportion. The key lies in the quality of touch.' (Gunter Nietsche, in *SD*, February, 1967.)

44, 45. Plan for the redevelopment of the Tsukiji quarter, 1966–7. Three-dimensional model seen from above, and in elevation. The building which appears on the far left is the model of the first design for the Dentsu Head Office building

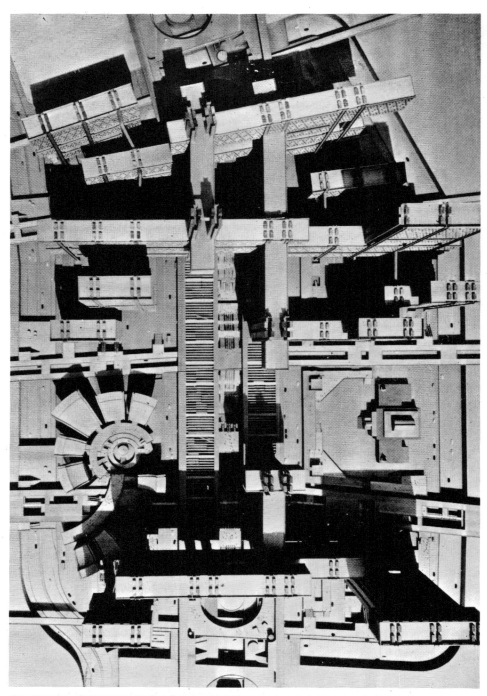

into the City Centre and a number of blocks and assigned the design responsibilities in several parts.

'The City Gate and the City Wall are the main elements from our competition proposal. The City Gate is a series region plan centred on a new train station and three interchanges from highways and containing a cluster of office buildings and Republic Square. The City Wall, located at the spot where the old city axis and the new city axis, emanating from the City Gate, come together, is an area surrounded by high-rise apartment buildings, which heightens the urbanity of the inner City Centre.

'If we ask what the thing is that gives structure to space we can answer that it is communication. Although we can consider that communication involves actual mobility, when things or people are in a state of flow, it is also possible to have visual communication in instances where nothing really moves. The process of formalising the communicational activities and flows within spaces is what we mean by "giving structure" to architectural or urban spaces. Although, until now, we have abstractly called spaces a place to live or a place to work, we cannot prescribe a space from such a static pattern alone. Going even farther, we find cases in which the spaces themselves are communicational fields, when we can give form to spaces as something symbolic.

'The channels of communication, in its many guises, are one of the foundations on which we give structure to the interior spaces of cities or vast complex buildings. We are sure that it is essential to revise our thinking to consider spaces as a communicational field.

'In our proposals for the international competitions for the World Health Organisation and in our design for the Kurashiki City Hall we gave structure to the whole by using spaces in this way—for visual communication—as core spaces, in other words. The dwelling unit that some MIT (Massachusetts Institute of Technology) students attempted and the housing groups over the sea in our Tokyo Plan, 1960, are examples of the same sort of thing. We gave structure to the two gymnasiums in the National Indoor Stadium complex through street architecture. Though a high-order traffic system gave structure to the entire civic axis of our Tokyo Plan, 1960, a network of elevated lattices with perpendicular roads gave structure to the forms of buildings to be built above that axis.

'The redevelopment proposal for the Tsukiji area in Tokyo was a more actualised version of the Tokyo Plan. Intensified vertical cores would carry people, information and energy upward. In accordance with necessity, we could build one of these cores after another and suspend bridge-like buildings between them. The system called for building core after core so that the whole would grow into three-dimensional lattices.'

The Communications Centre at Kofu comprises the main housing for mass communication media for the whole region—a radio station, the head offices of a newspaper, offices, and, on the ground floor, a section given over to shopping areas which serves the purpose of making link with the town itself. Perfect functionality and the possibility for further organic expansion of the various facilities were the criteria that Tange sought to satisfy in the new spatial arrangement based on the flow of communications.

The connecting links between the various units were first isolated and studied independently, then they were associated in order to assure the appropriate service of the various channels of communication. As a result, the overall distribution takes place vertically and is keyed to the three-dimensional lattice made up of the vertical core elements, which carry people, material, energy and information upwards, and whose location determines the interior functional arrangement of each individual floor.

So the usual arrangement of elevators, stairs, piping, electrical supplies, is reorganised, restructured and housed as a whole in the sixteen hollow cylinders, five metres in diameter, which also constitute the main structural support of the whole building. The maximum distance between supports is seventeen metres, and the absence of auxiliary supports in between ensures

46, 47 (following pages).
Aerial views of Kyoto and Tokyo in 1969. The two photographs provide a dramatic illustration of the extremes of change that Japanese urban centres are undergoing; while Kyoto still preserves a tradition layout, Tokyo has moved on to a confusion of anonymous construction brought about by speculation and the economic boom. In the centre of the second photograph, almost on a level with the horizon, one can see Kenzo Tange's Dentsu Building

Fig. 25

Pl. 51, Figs. 37, 43

the maximum flexibility in the space within the parallelepiped containers which bridge the gaps between the cylinders. The possibility of an organic development of the various parts according to a pre-established plan is guaranteed by the possibility for the construction of further core elements to support further containers. The open spaces between the cylinder core elements also provide a series of pedestrian areas on different levels that not only make a physical and visual separation between the various parts, but also make possible a certain amount of vertical expansion as well. The resulting impression, given sufficient implementation, makes the original formative concept quite obvious, and the actual profile of the buildings is pleasing even though its particular location does present some contrast of scale with the confinement of the site.

Tange himself was aware of this. 'This is an example of the way the three-dimensional space network operates in a single building,' he wrote, once again in the *Shinkenchiku* review. 'This is a proposal made up of architecture and urban design. There is certainly a problem of scale. The idea on which it is based would have no meaning in a small scale building; this in itself should constitute a criterion on which the scale of the structure is judged.'

Even if the building does go beyond the limits of such a critical standpoint and even if the scale is unsuitable for the point it seeks to make, the questions which is poses and the opportunities for experiment are a valuable contribution indeed. In this light the Kofu Communications Centre can be regarded as one of the most interesting designs in the whole of modern Japanese architecture. But this also circumscribes its value. The possibility of giving form to a particular moment of a process of development is a very enjoyable experience for an architect, but the human element of his architecture may suffer as a result.

After the Olympic stadiums and the Cathedral, where the inheritance of an outstanding figurative tradition is combined with the most advanced technological innovations, Tange shifts his emphasis once more from form to content and attempts a dialogue on an urban design level. This opened new possibilities for architects who although they had been engaged in a struggle on a cultural level that involved the whole social and technological system, on a practical level found themselves completely isolated.

The Kofu building is important in this connection also, coming as it does at such a critical moment in the country's history when the validity of all values and standards is being scrutinised and revised in all cultural spheres. For this reason some of the experiments are not being thrown out of hand merely because they involve risks.

The dawn of the future

Pls. 54–6

Tange's latest works continue to surprise us for their inventiveness and originality, for instance in the Head Office of the Shizuoka newspaper at Shimbashi (1967), whose structure is founded on the same principles as that of the Kofu Communications Centre. Here, however, it acquires polemical value, as well as contributing to urban design interpretation. The Asylum at Yukari (Tokyo, 1967) also contains methodological innovations.

Today Tange is engaged in a number of ambitious projects throughout the world. He is building a Sports and Arts Centre at Flushing Meadow, New York, a university campus at Taiwan, an airport on the Persian Gulf, and new administrative buildings in Bologna in Italy. In Japan he is working on the completion of a plan for Kyoto, and, together with the architects Kurokawa, Maki, Otaka, Isozaki and Kitutake, he has been designing the 1970 Osaka Expo.

It can thus be said that he has avoided static formulae for the expression of a very striking range of creations, which still maintain the freshness of their original conception. Tange is in a period of extraordinary creative inventiveness and the meaning of his contributions and their development is in large part assigned to his successors.

Tange's individuality does not lie, like that of the majority of the more famous Japanese architects, in a continual vindication of his own personality—it represents not a point of departure but a point of arrival. It is in this sense that we should be receptive to his propositions, as exhortations to follow him in a direction in which he believes, to an extent that goes far beyond facile enthusiasm. If we are dealing with monuments, these are the only kind of monuments that are acceptable to us in the modern town. If we are dealing with genius, this shows that genius is the result of a continuous and dedicated research that knows no compromise, rather than a revelation that suffices to fill an entire life. If anything, Tange shows us the way in which we can preserve this sort of value, even if in this respect he continues the great Japanese tradition of the past into the future.

But we should not forget that behind the traditions of the past there are the creative impulses which look towards the future. 'Today, the Japanese economy has been restructured,' says Tange,[28] 'and in step with it other institutions and social relationships have altered. And, what is most important, the Japanese people now look forward and not backward. We have entered a new era, the age of a technological civilisation, through which one can see a new transformed world in the future. We cannot find the solutions to our current problems simply by looking at the patterns of the past. Nor can the architect of this new society. He too must look ahead.'

It is as yet difficult to say what Tange's propositions will mean in terms of the solution to Japan's problems. The responsibility he bears is certainly enormous, as is the task that he has to undertake for himself in the revision of his original values, with no ambiguity, no compromise, standing firm in response to the demands made by production techniques and, equally, those presented by economic interests. He seeks above all to implement an unprecedentedly large constructional potential, confronting reality in its very essence, in the right dimensions, through an absolutely objective approach, thus fulfilling his job to the full.

28 Paolo Riani, *Architettura Giapponese contemporanea,* catalogue of the exhibition in Orsanmichele, Florence, 1969.

Colour plates

1

2

3

4

5

6

7

8

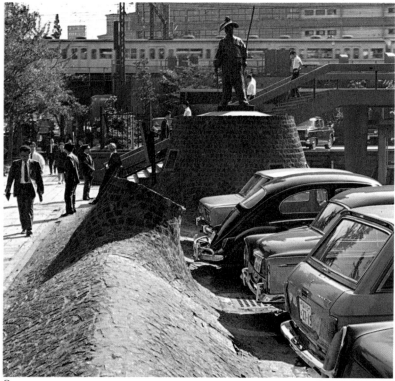

9

10

11

12

13

14

15

16

17

18

19

20

21

23

24

25

26

27

28

29

30

32

34

36

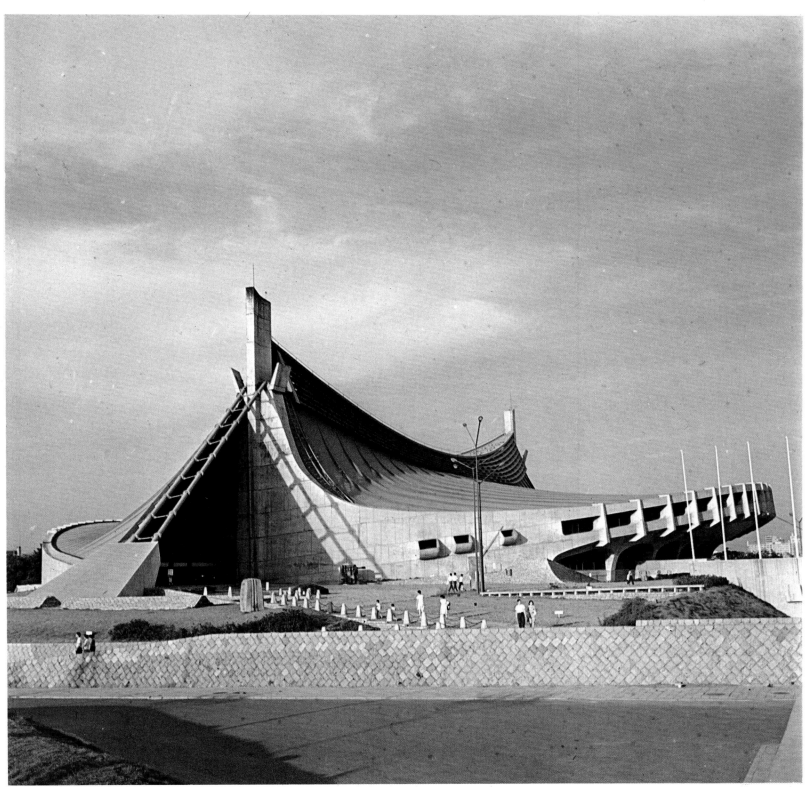

38

40

41

42

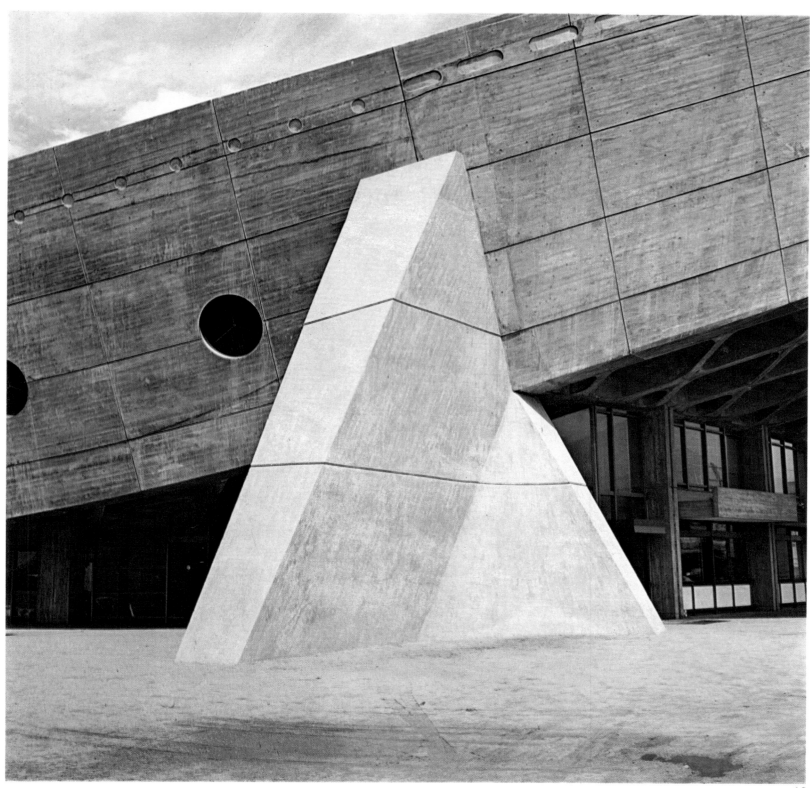

43

44

46

48

49

51

52

53

54

55

57

58

59

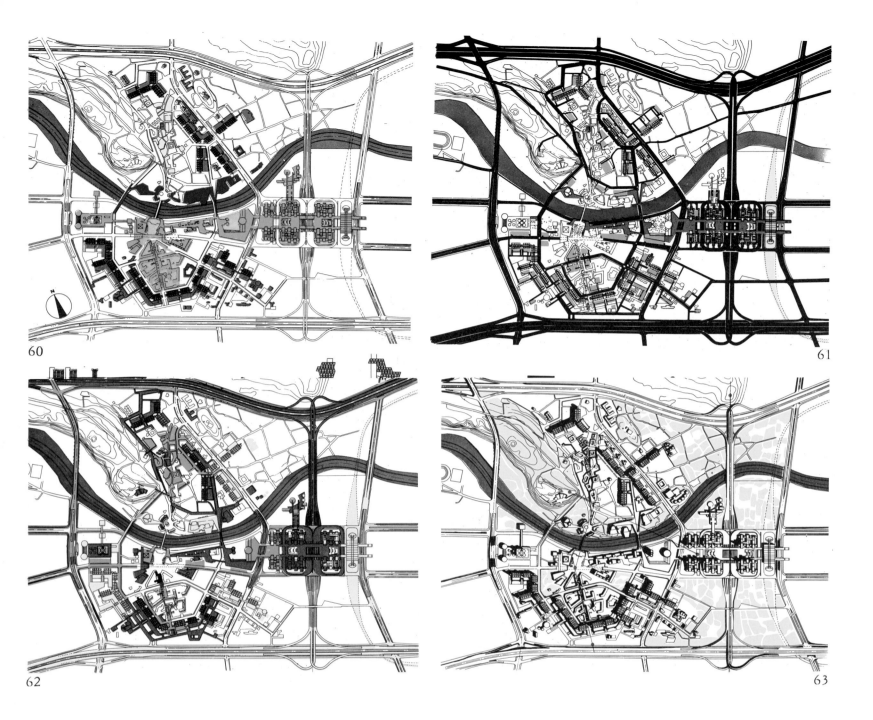

60

61

62

63

Description of colour plates

Biographical outline

1913. 4th November. Born in Osaka.

1935–8. Attended the Faculty of Architecture of Tokyo University.

1938. Was awarded the Tatsumo Prize for graduates of Tokyo University.

1938–41. Working in the studio of Kunio Mayekawa.

1941. Awarded the first prize for architecture (Nihon Kenchiku Gakkai).

1941–6. Research in Urban Design at Tokyo University.

1942. Wins first prize in the competition for the design of the Daitoa Kensetsu Memorial.

1943. Wins first prize in the competition for the Institute of Japanese Culture.

1946. Becomes an Assistant in architecture at Tokyo University.

1946–8. Plans for the reconstruction of the cities of Maebashi, Hiroshima, Isezaki.

1946. Second prize in the competitions for the reconstruction of the Ginza and Shinjuku quarters of Tokyo.

1947. Equal second prize for the reconstruction of a Roman Catholic chapel at Hiroshima.

1949. First prize in the competition for the Peace Park project and for the Peace Museum at Hiroshima.

1951. Becomes a member of the International Congress of Modern Architecture and attends its meeting in London.

1952. Wins first prize in the invitation competition for the Tokyo City Hall.

1954. Awarded the Annual Prize of the Japanese Institute of Architecture, for the Ehime Prefectural Office building. Works with Take, Ashihara, Ikebe and others.

1955. Awarded the Annual Prize of the Japanese Institute of Architecture for the Printing Press at Nomazu in the Shizuoka Prefecture.

1957. Awarded the Annual Prize of the Japanese Institute of Architecture for the Kurayoshi City Hall.

1960. Chairman of the World Design Congress in Tokyo. Together with Gropius and Ishimoto, publishes the book entitled *Katsura: Tradition and Creation in Japanese Architecture*. Participates in the competition for the United Nations building in Geneva. Becomes an honorary member of the Architects' Association of Mexico.

Awarded the prize of the Institute of Japanese Architecture for the Kagawa Prefectural Office.

1961. Publishes the *Plan for Tokyo*. Starts a private studio called URTEC.

1961–2. Together with other teachers, starts the course of Urban Engineering at Tokyo University.

1961–3. Collaborates on the plan for the areas of National Development.

1962. Receives an Honorary degree from the Fine Arts University, Buffalo. Publishes the book entitled *Ise: Prototype of Japanese Architecture* in collaboration with Noboru Kawazoe and Yoshio Watanahe.

1963. Receives an Honorary degree from Stuttgart University. Becomes Professor of Engineering at Tokyo University. Elected an honorary member of the International Architectural Association.

1964. Receives an Honorary degree from the University of Milan. Becomes a member of the International Committee for the Kennedy Memorial Library. Elected an honorary member of the Arts Academy in Germany. Awarded a diploma of merit by the IOC (International Olympic Committee) for the Olympic Stadiums in Tokyo. Publishes a study on the Tokaido Metropolis.

1965. Awarded the Asahisho Prize by the Asahi Shimbum newspaper for the Olympic Stadiums in Tokyo. Receives gold medal from RIBA (Royal Institute of British Architects). Elected an honorary member of the Peruvian Architects' Association. Awarded a special prize by the Japanese Institute of Architects for the Olympic Stadiums in Tokyo. Wins the first prize in the international invitation competition for the Skopje Reconstruction Plan (Yugoslavia).

1966. Awarded a special prize by the League of Architects of New York for the Olympic Stadiums in Tokyo. Elected to honorary membership of the American Arts Association. Awarded the gold medal of the International Architectural Association for his activity as an architect and town-planner.

48, 49. Kenzo Tange with some of his Western students

List of works

1941 Projects for residential units.

1942 Project for a Daitoa Kensetsu Memorial.

1943 Project for a building for the Japanese Institute of Culture.

1946–7 Plan for the reconstruction of the town of Hiroshima, in collaboration with Asada, Otani and Ishikawa.

1946–7 Plan for the reconstruction of the town of Maebashi, in collaboration with Asada and Otani.

1946 Plan for the reconstruction of the Ginza (Tokyo) in collaboration with Asada and Otani.

1946–7 Plan for the reconstruction of the town of Isezaki, in collaboration with Asada and Otani.

1946 Plan for the reconstruction of the Shinjuku quarter, in collaboration with Asada and Otani.

1947 Plan for the Fukushima area, in collaboration with Take, Ikebe, Asada, Otani and others.

1947–8 Plan for the redevelopment of the Hongo Bunkyo area of Tokyo in collaboration with Takayama, Ikebe, Asada and Otani.

1947 Plan for the town of Wakkanai, in collaboration with Asada and Otani.

1947 Plan for the Peace Centre at Hiroshima, in collaboration with Kiyoda, Otani and Asada.

1949 Exhibition on the reconstruction of Japanese towns, in collaboration with Joshizaka, Take, Ikebe, Asada, Otani.

1949 Pavilion for the Foreign Exchange Exhibition.

1949–51 Peace Park at Hiroshima, in collaboration with Asada, Otani and others.

1949–55 Museum in the Peace Centre at Hiroshima, in collaboration with Asada, Otani and others.

1949–53 Project for the Auditorium of the Peace Centre at Hiroshima, in collaboration with Asada, Otani and others.

1949 Project for a Shopping Centre in the Ginza (Tokyo) in collaboration with Asada, Ozuki, Otani and others.

1949 Project for the Aquarium of the Ueno (Tokyo) Zoo, in collaboration with Asada, Ozuki, Otani and others.

1949 Takes part in the Shinseisaku Competition (Tokyo).

1950 Pavilion at the Japanese Foreign Trade Exhibition in collaboration with Asada, Otani and Kawai. Project for the Radio building at Nagoia.

1951–3 Children's Library at Hiroshima, in collaboration with Asada, Oki, Ozuki, Otani, Mitsuyoshi and others.

1952–3 Conference Centre at Matsuyama, the Ehime Prefectural Office in collaboration with Asada, Tarashima, Oki, Ozuki, Otani, Mitsuyoshi.

1952 Project for the Auditorium of the Provincial Library at Kagawa, in collaboration with Asada, Otani, Oki, Ozuki, Kawai, Mitsuyoshi, Kamiya.

1952–3 Builds his own house in Tokyo.

1952 Project for the Foreign Ministry, in collaboration with Otani, Oki, Ozuki, Maki, Tarashima, Mitsuyoshi, Kamiya.

1952–7 City Hall, Tokyo, in collaboration with Asada, Otani, Mitsuyoshi, Kamiya, Ozuki, Ki.

1953–4 Library of Tsudajuku University, in collaboration with Kamiya and Nayashima.

1953–4 Shimizu City Hall, in collaboration with Kamiya, Ozuki, Asada, Mitsuyoshi and others.

1954 Exhibition at Shinodatoko. Project for the Parliament Library, in collaboration with Ozuki, Otani, Asada.

1954–5 Printing Press at Numazu Shizuoka, in collaboration with Oki, Asada, Yamasaki and others.

1955–7 Kurayoshi City Hall, in collaboration with Kishida and others.

1955–8 Kagawa Prefectural Hall, in collaboration with Oki, Asada, Kamiya and others. Project for the group of buildings around the Tokyo City Hall, in collaboration with Isozaki and Kurokawa.

1956–8 Sogetsu Art Centre, in collaboration with Nagashima, Okamura and others.

1956–7 Sumi Memorial Hall, in collaboration with Kimura, Soshi, Saito and others.

1956–7 Sports Centre at Shizuoka, in collaboration with Ozuki, Yoshioka and others.

1957–8 Auditorium at Imabari (Ehime), in collaboration with Mogi, Isozaki and others.

1958 Plan for the city of Toronto (Canada) in collaboration with Asada, Otani, Kimura, Nagashima, Yoshikawa, Nishihara, Isozaki, Okamura, Yoshioka, Sugi, Inazuka, Soshi and others.

1957–60 Offices for the Dentsu Advertising Co. in Osaka, in collaboration with Otani, Sugi, Kimura, Watanabe.

1957–60 Kurashiki City Hall, in collaboration with Nishihara, Yoshioka.

1957–61 Atami Garden Hotel, in collaboration with Inazuka, Nagashima and others.

1957–60 Library for Rikkyo University, in collaboration with Inazuka, Kamiya and Isozaki.

1959–60 Project for the Offices of the Kokuyo in Tokyo, in collaboration with Yoshikawa and Yoshioka.

1958–60 Shinyokinko Office building in Imabari, in collaboration with Akui, Soshi, Isozaki and others.

1959–64 Residential areas in Takamatsu, in collaboration with Kamiya, Kurokawa and others.

1959–60 Project for a community of 25,000 in Boston Bay.

1960 Project for WHO (World Health Organisation) in Geneva, in collaboration with Kamiya, Kimura, Nagashima, Okamura, Yoshioka, Watanabe, Akui, Inazuka, Sone.

1960–1 Gold Club at Totsuka, in collaboration with Soshi, Sone and the URTEC Team.

1962–3 Bank in Saitama, in collaboration with Yoshioka, Soshi and others.

1960–3 Cultural Centre in Nichinan, in collaboration with Kimura and others.

1961–4 Swimming Pool and Sports Centre for the 1964 Olympic Games in Tokyo, in collaboration with Kamiya, Nagashima, Yoshioka, Kimura, Watanabe, Okamura, Yamamoto, Sasaki, Helena and Israel Gotovic, Inazuka, Ejiri Soshi, Sone, Ko, the University Institute, and URTEC.

1962–4 Sports Centre in Takamatsu, with the URTEC Team and the Shudansesaku Architectural Office.

1963–4 St Mary's Catholic Cathedral in Tokyo, with the URTEC Team, in collaboration with Soshi, Kamiya, Sasaki and others.

1963–4 Factory for the Shikkin Ent. K.K. in Gifu, with the URTEC Team, in collaboration with Kamiya, Sone, and Hiraga.

1964–5 Public building at Imabari, with the URTEC Team, and in collaboration with Kamiya and Hiraga.

1965–6 Service Station and Restaurant on the Menshijn Motorway, with the URTEC Team and in collaboration with Kamiya, Watanabe, Kimura, Doki.

1965–7 Project for the reconstruction of the City of Skopje (Yugoslavia) in collaboration with Isozaki, Watanabe, Mutsushita and others.

1966–7 Project for the redevelopment of the Tsukiji area of Tokyo, in collaboration with Kamiya, Kimura, Watanabe and others.

1967–8 Head Office of the Shizuoka Newspaper and Broadcasting Company (Tokyo) with the URTEC Team.

1967–8 Head Office of the Dentsu Advertising Company (Tokyo) with the URTEC Team.

1967–70 Plan for the Osaka 1970 World's Fair, in collaboration with Isozaki, Kikutake, Otaka, Kurokawa and others.

Bibliography

The industrial revolution and the social upheaval which accompanies it have been in Japan a reality that has emerged suddenly into the context of a traditional pattern of life that has remained intact and active right to the present day.

In order to comprehend it, it is essential to have an understanding of the civilisation into which it has emerged.

In view of the extent of the material, the reader is referred to the bibliographical survey prepared by Paolo Riani, in the catalogue of the exhibition 'Architettura giapponese contemporanea' (Contemporary Japanese Architecture) held in Orsanmichele in Florence from 15th March to 15th April, 1969 (Edizioni Centro Di, Florence, 1969).

BOOKS AND WRITINGS BY KENZO TANGE

'Creation in Present-day Architecture and The Japanese Architectural Tradition', *New Architecture of Japan*, June, 1956; 'The Architect in Japan–His Outer World and His Inner World', *New Architecture of Japan*, October, 1956; 'Shizuoka Kongresshalle', *Bauwelt*, Berlin, 9th June, 1958; 'A Central Core for the World's Largest City', *New Architecture of Japan*, June, 1958; 'Integrated Plan for the Tokyo Metropolitan Government Building' (with the Kenzo Tange Team), *New Architecture of Japan*, June, 1958; 'An Approach to Tradition', *The Japan Architect*, 2nd January, 1959; 'Hotel de Ville de Tokyo', *L'Architecture d'Aujourd'hui*, 3rd February, 1959; 'Prefecture de Kagawa à Takamatsu', *L'Architecture d'Aujourd'hui*, 7th June, 1959; 'In Greeting World Design Conference', *Kindai Kentiku*, May, 1960; 'Kurashiki City Hall', *The Japan Architect*, October, 1960; 'Katsura–Tradition and Creation in Japanese Architecture' (with Gropius and Ishimoto), New Haven, Yale University Press; 'Technology and Humanity', *Architectural Design*, February, 1961; 'A Plan for Tokyo, 1960–Toward a Structural Reorganization' (with the Kenzo Tange Team), *The Japan Architect*, April, 1961; 'A Plan for Tokyo, 1960' (official report), Tokyo, 1961; 'A Building and a Project', *Ekistics*; 'Der neue CIAM', *Bauen + Wohnen*, July 1961; 'Hôtel de Ville de Kurashiki' (in collaboration), *L'Architecture d'Aujourd'hui*, October, 1961; 'Architecture-City', *Contemporary Architecture of the World*, 1961, Shokokusha Publishing Co., 1961; 'Un Piano per Tokyo', *Casabella*, No. 258, Milan, December, 1961; 'Integration between Architecture and Art', *Pioneering in Art Collecting*, published by Albright-Knox Art Gallery, Buffalo, New York, 1962; 'Ein Plan für Tokio', *Bauen + Wohnen*, July, 1962; 'Plano de urbanizacão para Toquio', *Binario-Arquitectura Construcão, Equipamento 52*, Lisbon, 1963; 'The future of Tokyo', *Orient–West Magazine*, 1963; 'Ein Plan für Tokyo', *Bauen + Wohnen*, 1963; 'Gymnase National de Yoyogi', *L'Architecture d'Aujourd'hui*, September, 1964; 'Architecture et urbanisme au XXe siècle'–'Le stade national de Tokyo', *L'Oeil*, 122 (special issue), Paris, 1965; 'Ise–Prototype of Japanese Architecture', MIT Press, Cambridge (Massachusetts), 1965; 'Skopje Urban Plan' (official report), Skopje, 1965; 'Urbanization and Japanese culture', *Bulletin 10th anniversary issue*, The International House of Japan Inc., 1965; 'Zum Entwurf der Sporthalle in Tokyo', *Bauen + Wohnen*, October, 1965; 'Le Corbusier, art et architecture', October, 1965; 'Le Corbusier', *Progressive Architecture*, November, 1965; 'Le Corbusier: témoignage', *Aujourd'hui*, November, 1965; 'Projet pour le centre de radio diffusion Yamanashi', *L'Architecture d'Aujourd'hui*, September, 1966; 'Gymnase de Kagawa', *L'Architecture d'Aujourd'hui*, September, 1966; 'Le Plan-Maître de l'Exposition Japonaise Universelle Internationale, Osaka 1970' (official report), 1968.

HISTORIES OF ARCHITECTURE AND SURVEYS

H. R. HITCHCOCK, *Architecture XIX–XX Century*, New York, 1958; S. TAKIGUCHI, 'Giappone', *Enciclopedia Universale dell'Arte*, vol. VI, Florence, 1960; L. BENEVOLO, *Storia dell'Architettura moderna*, Bari, 1960; U. KULTERMANN, *Architecture nouvelle au Japon*, Paris, 1960; B. CHAMPIGNEULLE, J. ACHE, *L'Architecture du XXe siècle*, Paris, 1962; H. KISHIDA, *Japanese Architecture*, J.T.B., Tokyo; J. M. RICHARDS, *An Architectural Journey in Japan*, London, 1963; M. TAFURI, *L'Architettura Moderna in Giappone*, Bologna, 1964; K. NOBORU, *Contemporary Japanese Architecture*, Japanese Life and Culture Series, K.B.S.,Tokyo, 1965, 1968; JAPAN ARCHITECTS ASSOCIATION, *Japanese Architecture, Guide to East Japan; Japanese Architecture, Guide to West Japan*, Publication Bureau of Asahi Shimbur, Tokyo; R. BOYD, *New Directions in Japanese Architecture*, G. Braziller, New York, 1968; P. RIANI, *Architettura Giapponese Contemporanea*, Catalogue of the Exhibition in Orsanmichele, Florence, Ed. Centro DI, 1969.

MONOGRAPHS

R. BOYD, 'Kenzo Tange–Makers of contemporary architecture', George Braziller, New York, Prentice-Hall International, London, ID., 'Kenzo Tange', I. Saggiatore, Milan, 1963, a view of Tange's work up to 1962; contains some useful notes, a short critical introduction, and a few of Tange's writings (in Italian); 'Kenzo Tange, 1949–1965 Exhibition', The American Federation of Art, 1966–7, New York; K. TANGE, 'Genjitsu to Sozo', 1946, 1958, Bijitsu Shuppansho, Tokyo, 1966; K. TANGE, 'Gijitsu no Ningen', 1955, 1964, Bijitsu Shuppansho, Tokyo, 1967, 2 volume work including all Tange's work, edited by the architect himself (in Japanese); A. ALTHER, 'Three Japanese Architects: Mayekawa, Tange, Sakakura', Teufen, 1968. (Review of the work of the three architects up to 1968 made by a Swiss architect who has been in touch with the world of Japan since 1930. Brief commentaries, and good photographic coverage.)

ARTICLES

'Kenzo Tange–Giappone modernissimo', *Domus*, Milan, April, 1952; 'Architect Tange Builds for Community's Needs', *Nippon Times*, July, 1954; E. GRILLI, 'Calligraphy and Abstraction', *Nippon Times*, 17th September, 1954; 'Two triumphs of space in Japan–Kenzo Tange', *Architectural Forum*, 1955; T. ASADA, 'Hiroshima Plan (1946–1955)–final report on the Peace Center', *New Architecture of Japan*, June, 1956; G. PERRIAND, 'Crisi del gesto in Giappone', *Casabella Continuità*, No. 210, 1956; PERRIAND, IKEBE, BELMONT, MURATA, KANO, 'Varia', *L'architecture d'Aujourd'hui*, No. 65, 1956; V.G., 'Il Centro della Pace ad Hiroshima di Kenzo Tange', *Casabella Continuità*, No. 212, 1956; 'Kurayoshi City Hall', *New Architecture of Japan*, July, 1957; 'An architect's home near Tokyo', *International Asbestos–Cement Review*, Zurich, October, 1957; M. B. BLOCH, 'Eget hus is Tokio', *Arkitektur*, Copenhagen, June–July, 1958; H. ZACHERT, 'Blick nach Japan', *Bauwelt*, Berlin, 9th June, 1958; I. KAWAHARA, 'Tre problemi del' architettura giapponese', *Sele-Arte*, No. 36, 1958; C. SIEGEL, 'Ein Beitrag zur Kongresshallen-Debatte', *Bauwelt*, Berlin, 9th June, 1958; 'Kenzo Tange', *L'Architecture d'Aujourd'hui*, 7th June, 1958; 'Kenzo Tange–a Japanese architect seeks a new expression', *Architectural Record*, July, 1958; 'Organico giapponese? Ufficia Shizuoka', *L'Architectura*, July, 1958; 'L'Auditorium Municipale di Shizuoka, in Giappone', *L'Architettura*, July, 1958; U. KULTERMANN, 'Neues Bauen in Japan', Verlag Ernst Wasmuth, Tübingen, 1958; ID., 'Baukunst der Gegenwart', Verlag Ernst Wasmuth, Tübingen, 1958; 'Tokyo's controversial City Hall–A continuing review of international building', *Architectural Forum*, September, 1958; 'The Sogetsu Art Centre', *New Architecture of Japan*, October, 1958; N. KAWAZOE, 'Modern Japanese Architecture Confronts Functionalism', *Zodiac*, No. 3; 'Houses Architects Live in: the New and Old in Japan', *Life*, 19th January, 1959; U. KULTERMANN, 'Die Versammlungshalle in Shizuoka', *Die Innenarchitectur*, Essen, January, 1959; P. BLAKE, 'What is Government Character?', *Architectural Forum*, January, 1959; N. KAWAZOE, 'Kenzo Tange', *The Japan Architect*, 2nd January, 1959; K. KAMIYA, 'Comments on the Kagawa Prefectural Office', *The Japan Architect*, 2nd January, 1959; Y. KOJIRO, 'Japanese Architecture in 1958–New Vitality', *The Japan Architect*, 2nd January, 1959; U. KULTERMANN, 'Kenzo Tange's forsamlingshal i Shizuoka', *Arkitektur*, Denmark, February, 1959; 'Kagawa prefectural office–Kenzo Tange', *The Japan Architect*, 2nd January, 1959; 'News and comments–Kenzo Tange', *The Japan Architect*, May, 1959; C. TERRY, 'Kenzo Tange–no friend of tradition', *Japan Quarterly*, vol. 6, No. 2, 1959; 'A Central Core for the Tokyo City', *The Japan Architect*, June, 1959; 'Kenzo Tange–Premier Grand Prix International d'Architecture et d'Art de l'Architecture d'Aujourd'hui, *L'Architecture d'Aujourd'hui*, 7th June, 1959; 'Musées et Centres d'Art–Centre d'Art de Sogetsu, Tokio', *Aujourd'hui*, June, 1959; R. BOURNE, 'Renaissance in Japan', *Forum*, September, 1959; *Architectural Forum*, issue devoted exclusively to Tange, 1959; 'Tange's Popular Prefecture Office', *Forum*, September, 1959; K. MOGI, 'Imabari City Hall and Public Hall', *The Japan Architect*, October, 1959; B. ZEVI, 'Un giapponese contro la tradizione (Kenzo Tange)', *L'Espresso*, No. 38, 1959; 'Osaka Dentsu Building', *The Japan Architect*, October, 1959; T. IKUTA, 'On the Osaka Dentsu Building', *The Japan Architect*, 1959; K. HIGUCHI, 'On Seeing the Osaka Dentsu Building', *The Japan Architect*, October, 1959; 'Ornamented Modern e Brutalism: Verso due movimenti?', *Zodiac*, No. 4, 1959; 'New Japanese Architect', *Time*, 30th November, 1959; 'Palazzo Municipale di Kurayoshi', *Edilizia Moderna*, No. 68, Milan; 'Sumi Memorial Hall', *Edilizia Moderna*, No. 68, Milan; 'Shizuoka Convention Hall', *Edilizia Moderna*. No. 68. Milan; G. KOLLANDSRUD, 'Kenzo Tange', *Byggekunst*, No. 2, Norway; W. GROPIUS, 'Architecture in Japan', *Yale Architectural Journal*, December, 1959; 'Work of Kenzo Tange', *Annual of Architecture Structure and Town Planning*, The Publishing Corporation India; U. KULTERMANN, 'Bauen in Japan–Kenzo Tange', *Bauen + Wohnen*, Munich/Zurich, January, 1960; 'Municipality of Kurashiki–Kenzo Tange', *The Japan Architect*, November, 1960; 'CIAM–Kenzo Tange', *The Japan Architect*, November, 1960; W. GROPIUS, 'Kenzo Tange–and the question of our tradition', *The Auburn Alumi News*, February, 1960; C. TOWERY, 'Architettura in Giappone', *Architettura*, No. 33, Milan; 'Otterlo 1959 Statement by Kenzo Tange', *Architectural Design*, May, 1960; 'Architects Place Great Hopes on the Conference's Outcome', *Asahi Evening News*, July, 1960; M. NOVOTNEJ, 'Japonska architecktura', *Novy Orient* (New Orient), Prague, August, 1960; W. GROPIUS, 'Architettura in Giappone', *Architettura cantiere*, No. 13, 1960; 'Panorama 1960–Hôtel de Ville d'Imabari, Japon', *L'Architecture d'Aujourd'hui*, 10th September, 1960; 'Architecture and Urbanism–Aestheticism and Vitalism, Technology and Humanity, a Building and Project', *The Japan Architect*, October, 1960; U. KULTERMANN, 'Kenzo Tange–Genius Japans', *Das Kunstwerk*, Baden-Baden, 12th November, 1960; 'Sede dell'Organizzazione Mondiale della Sanita Ginevra, Concorso', *L'Architettura*, No. 62, 6th year; U. KULTERMANN, 'Neues Bauen in Japan', Verlag Ernst Wasmuth, Tübingen; W. GROPIUS, K. TANGE, Y. ISHIMOTO, 'Katsura–Tradition and Creation in Japanese Architecture', Yale University Press, New Haven; 'Kurashiki Town Hall', *Architectural Review*, January, 1961; 'Palazzo Comunale, Kurashiki', *L'Architettura*, No. 63, 6th year; ALISON & PETER SMITHSON, 'The Rebirth of Japanese Architecture', *Architectural Design*, February, 1961; 'Dialogue Questions by Kenzo Tange and answers by Antonin Raymond', *Architectural Design*, February, 1961; M. TAFURI, 'Un piano per Tokyo e le nuove problematiche dell'urbanistica contemporanea; panorama', *Argomenti di Architettura*, No. 4, 1961; J. E. BURCHARD, 'New Currents in Japanese Architecture–Kenzo Tange', *Architectural Record*, New York, April, 1961; C. JONES, 'Making Something New of Tradition, Kenzo Tange', *Horizon*; 'Hall commémoratif Sumi', *L'Architecture d'Aujourd'hui*, October, 1961; 'Immeuble Dentsu', *L'Architecture d'Aujourd'hui*, October, 1961; 'Project pour un plan d'urbanisme de Tokyo', *L'Architecture d'Aujourd'hui*, October, 1961; 'Piano regolatore di Tokyo, Progetto', *L'Architettura*, No. 72, 7th year; K. KAMIYA, 'New Architecture in an

Old Environment', *The Japan Architect*, November, 1961; G. GRASSI, 'La Città, come prestazione vitale', *Casabella*, No. 258, Milan, December, 1961; C. JONES, 'Kenzo Tange–The Meeting of East and West', *Architecture today and tomorrow*, New York; O. NEWMAN, 'CIAM '59 in Otterlo–Kenzo Tange, Tokyo, Japan', Karl Kramer Verlag, Stuttgart, Verlag Girsberger, Zurich, Alec Tiranti Ltd., London, Universe Book Inc., New York; U. G. VAN SAANE, 'Lectura Architectonica', Hilversum; PH. THIEL, 'City Hall at Kurashiki, Japan', *The Architectural Review*, No. 780, February, 1962; 'Nichinan cultural centre', *The Japan Architect*, February, 1962; 'P/A Talks with Kenzo Tange', *Progressive Architecture*, March, 1962; B. ZEVI, 'Costruiranno la capitale sulle Palafitte', *L'Espresso*, March, 1962; 'Golfhaus Totsuka bei Tokyo', *Bauen + Wohnen*, Zurich, June, 1962; C. S. TERRY, 'The Atami Garden Hotel', *The Japan Architect*, June, 1962; J. M. RICHARDS, 'Japan 1962', *The Architectural Review*, No. 787, September, 1962; 'Albergo ad Atami presso Tokyo', *L'Architettura*, No. 83, 8th year, 'A Plan for Tokyo', *Forum*, No. 2, Amsterdam, 1962; C. COULIN, 'Architekten Zeichnen', Stuttgart, 1962; M. MANIERI-ELIA, 'Dal piani aperto alla città-regione (sul piano di Tokyo)', *Ing. arch. i*, Nos. 2–3, 1962; N. KAWAZOE, 'Propositions d'Urbanisme en Japon', *L'Architecture d'Aujourd'hui*, No. 101, 1962; J. M. RICHARDS, 'Japan 1962', *Architectural Review*, No. 787, 1962; 'Hôtel à Atami, Japon', *L'Architecture d'Aujourd'hui*, December, 1962; 'Club de Golf à Totsuka près de Tokio', *L'Architecture d'Aujourd'hui*, December, 1962; TARO-AMANO, 'Golf-club presso Tokyo', *L'Architettura cronache e storia*, No. 89, March, 1963; 'Project pour la *Cathédrale de Tokio*', *L'Architecture d'Aujourd'hui*, 7th June, 1963; CALCHI NOVATI, INAGAKI, TAJIMA, ASTI, various articles in the issue devoted to Japan, *Casabella-Continuità*, No. 273, 1963; 'Il Grattacielo–Kenzo Tange: un piano per Tokyo–Sistema Midollare', *Edilizia Moderna*, September, 1963; A. F. ALBA, Kenzo Tange, *Arquitectura*, No. 60, Madrid, 1963; P. BLAKE, 'Five shapers of today's skyline', *The New York Times Book Review*, 1963; M. MAYERSON, 'Memorial Peace Centre, Hiroshima', *Face of the Metropolis*, New York, 1963; 'National Gymnasium', *The Japan Architect*, June, 1963; 'Totsuka golf club house', *The Japan Architect*, January, 1963; G. HATJIE, 'Kenzo Tange', *Encyclopaedia of Modern Architecture*, London; J. M. RICHARDS, 'An architectural journey in Japan', *The Architectural Press*, London; J. JOEDICKE, 'Utopie und Realität in der Stadtplanung', *Bauen + Wohnen*, 1963; 'Nationale Sporthallen Tokio', *Bauen + Wohnen*, 1963; O. MARC, 'Japon: L'architecture japonaise des origines à nos jours', *Aujourd'hui*, No. 44, January, 1964; V. KENRICK, 'Kenzo Tange personality profile', *The Japan Times*, 24th March, 1964; 'Latà Città e come un atomo e noi siamo gli elettroni', *Il Diario de Milano*, 5th April, 1964; 'Tokyo Olympics Indoor Swimming Pool Building–Architect Tange Awarded Olympic Diploma of Merit', *Japan in Pictures*, vol. 6, No. 6, 1964; S. WADA, 'Hotel Atami Garden, Japan', *Moebel Interior Design*, June, 1964; ID., 'Nichinan Cultural Centre, Japan', *Moebel Interior Design*; 'Clean Sweep in Olympics', *Architectural Forum*, 9th August, 1964; A.B., 'Jeux Olympiques Tokyo 1964 et Constructions Sportives', *L'Architecture d'Aujourd'hui*, 11th September, 1964; P. SMITHSON, 'Reflection on Kenzo Tange's Tokyo Bay Plan', *Architectural Design*, London, October, 1964; 'The approach of the Kenzo Tange Team in their plan . for Tokyo 1960', *Architectural Design*, London, October, 1964; J. C. ROWAN, 'The Future of Urban Environment', *Progressive Architecture*, New York, October, 1964; 'On the National Gymnasium–Kenzo Tange', *The Japan Architect*, November, 1964; 'The National Gymnasium and Annex–Kenzo Tange', *The Japan Architect*, November, 1964; 'Urban Design for Kenzo Tange must seek to reconcile the discrepancy between mass-human scale of the technology and the scale of Man' and 'Tokyo Cathedral', *Liturgical Arts*, vol. 32, No. 4, New York; H. SASAKI, 'Architecture for the Tokyo Olympic Games', *Japan Design House*, 1964; 'Kenzo Tange Kulturzentrum Nichinan', *Bauen + Wohnen* II, 1964; J. JOEDICKE, 'New Brutalism', *Bauen + Wohnen* II, 1964; S. DIBBLE, 'Spectacular New Cathedral for Tokyo and an Architect with Vision', *The Japan Times*, 23rd December, 1964; J.T.B. jun., 'Big Tops by Tange at Tokyo Olympics', *Progressive Architecture*, December, 1964; K. TANGE, Y. ASHIHARA, 'Progetti per le Olimpiadi di Tokyo', *L'Architettura cronache e storia*, No. 105, July, 1964; VOCE, 'Kenzo Tange', *Encyclopedia of modern architecture*, Harry H. Abrams, New York; H. RAHMS, 'Eine Kathedrale in Tokyo – Der Japanische Architekt Kenzo Tange in Köln', *Frankfurter Allgemeine*, 14th April, 1965; 'Kenzo Tange', *Concrete Quarterly*, Cement and Concrete Association, London, 1965; J. DODD, Japanese Architecture Today', *Architectural Design*, March, 1965; G. NIETSCHE, 'Japan's second heroic age–The age of barbarism', *Architectural Design*, March, 1965; 'A Kenzo Tange la medaglia d'oro del RIBA', *L'Architettura cronache e storia*, No. 114, April, 1965; N. HOZUMI and J. DODD, 'Kenzo Tange', *Architectural Design*, March, 1965; J. DONAT, 'Kenzo Tange', *World Architecture 2*, Studio Vista, London; R. BOYD, 'A Cruciform Window onto Heaven', *Architectural Forum*, New York, September, 1965; 'K. Tange, Cattedrale cattolica a Tokyo', *L'Architettura cronache e storia*, No. 121, November, 1965; M. CLERICI, 'Impianti sportivi per le Olimpiadi di Tokyo di Kenzo Tange', *L'Architettura cronache e storia*, No. 114, April, 1965; 'K. Tange, Plastico per la ricostruzione del quartiere Tsukiji, Tokyo; Plastico per il palazzo degli uffici Dentsu; Plastico per il centro radiofonico di Yamanashi, *L'Architettura e storia*, No. 117, July, 1965; 'Tokyo Saint Mary's Cathedral–Kenzo Tange', *The Japan Architect*, August, 1965; 'The Kagawa Prefectural Gymnasium–Kenzo Tange', *The Japan Architect*, August, 1965; JOE, 'Aufbau der Konstruktion', *Bauen + Wohnen*, October, 1965; Stadtverweiterung Tokio', *Haus und Wohnung*, Frankfurt, November, 1965; PZ, 'Kulturzentrum Nichinan (Prafektur Miyazaki', *Bauen + Wohnen*, November, 1965; 'Kenzo Tange', *Architectural Design*, December, 1965; 'Kenzo Tange–Marien Kathedrale von Tokio', *Bauen + Wohnen*, December, 1965; S. WADA, 'Saint Mary's Cathedral Tokyo', *Moebel Interior Design*, December, 1965; R. BOYD, 'The Puzzle of Architecture', Cambridge University Press, London and New York, 1965; 'The plan of Skopje', *Architectural Review*, January, 1966; U.S., 'Kathedrale in Tokio', *Baumeister*, February, 1966, Callwey, Munich; 'Olympic Building', *Architectural Review*, April, 1966; 'The 1st Japan Art Festival', Japan Art Festival Association, 1966; G. NIETSCHE, 'The Japanese Sense of "Place" in old and new architecture and planning', *Architectural Design*, June, 1966; R. HAMAGUCHI, 'History of Modern Architecture 20 Years after War', *The Japan Architect*, June, 1966; H. ONOBAYASHI, 'Chronological Table of Modern Japanese Architecture 1945–1965', *The Japan Architect*, June, 1966; R. BOYD, 'Kenzo Tange, An Architect of the World', *A.I.A. Journal*, June, 1966; 'Kenzo Tange e Bologna', *Chiesa e Quartiere*, Bologna, December, 1966; 'Kenzo Tange on Residential Design', *The Japan Architect*, March, 1966; L. M. BOSCHINI and M. MITROVIC, 'Il concorso per il centro di Skopje', *Casabella*, No. 307, 1966; P. RIANI, 'Un vulcano di cementol', *Pirelli–rivista d'informazione e di technica*, No. 4, 1967; 'Panoramica dell'Expo '67', *L'Architettura cronache e storia*, No. 141, July, 1967; 'Piano di massima per l'Esposizione 1970 a Osaka', *L'Architettura cronache e storia*, 141, July, 1967; 'K. Tange, Palazzo della stampa e della radio per la citta di Yamanashi', *L'Architettura cronache e storia*, No. 143, September, 1967; 'K. Tange, Progetto vincitore del Concorso per la ricostruzione di Skopje', *L'Architettura cronache e storia*, No. 145, November, 1967; 'K. Tange, Progetto per il quartiere Tsukiji a Tokyo', *L'Architettura cronache e storia*, No. 146, December, 1967; P. RIANI, 'Un edificio a Kofu di Kenzo Tange', *L'Arquitetura*, 1967; 'K. Tange, Giardino d'infanzia a Yukari', *L'Architettura cronache e storia*, No. 148, February, 1968; 'The Winners of the Shinkenchiku 1966 Residential Design Competition–Kenzo Tange', *The Japan Architect*, 1st February, 1967; 'The Yamanashi Communication Centre–Kenzo Tange', *The Japan Architect*, May, 1967; 'Skopje Urban Plan–Kenzo Tange', *The Japan Architect*, May, 1967; 'A Plan for the Tokyo Tsukiji Area–Kenzo Tange', *The Japan Architect*, May, 1967; 'The Tokiwamachi Branch of the Imabari Trust Bank–Kenzo Tange', *The Japan Architect*, November, 1967; 'The Shizuoka Newspaper and Broadcasting Co.–Kenzo Tange', *The Japan Architect*, April, 1968; 'Main Office of the Dentsu Advertising Co., Kenzo Tange', *The Japan Architect*, April, 1968; P. RIANI, 'Il divenire nella citta giapponese', *Casabella*, No. 326, 1968; 'K. Tange e URTEC, Sede del quotidiano Shizuoka a Tokyo', *L'Architettura cronache e storia*, No. 155, September, 1968; 'Tokyo's flatiron Building', *Architectural Forum*, March, 1968; J. M. RICHARDS, 'Preview: Osaka '70', *The Architectural Review*, No. 862, November, 1968.